Archibald Lampman

Twayne's World Authors Series

Canadian Literature

Robert Lecker, Editor

McGill University

TWAS 770

ARCHIBALD LAMPMAN
(1861–1899)
Reproduction made with permission
from an original held in Special Collection,
The Library, Simon Fraser University,
Burnaby, British Columbia

Archibald Lampman

By L. R. Early

York University

Twayne Publishers • Boston

Archibald Lampman

L. R. Early

Copyright © 1986 by G.K. Hall & Co.
All Rights Reserved
Published by Twayne Publishers
A Division of G.K. Hall & Co.
70 Lincoln Street
Boston, Massachusetts 02111

Copyediting supervised by Lewis DeSimone
Book production by Elizabeth Todesco
Book design by Barbara Anderson

Typeset in 11 pt. Garamond
by Modern Graphics, Inc., Weymouth, Massachusetts

Printed on permanent/durable acid-free paper
and bound in the United States of America

Library of Congress Cataloging in Publication Data

Early, L. R.
 Archibald Lampman.

 (Twayne's world authors series. Canadian literature)
 Bibliography: p. 164
 Includes index.
 1. Lampman, Archibald, 1861–1899—Criticism and
interpretation. I. Title II. Series.
PR9199.2.L3Z66 1986   811'.4   85–21929
ISBN 0–8057–6621–9

This book is for my parents,
William Edward Early
Irene Frith Early

Contents

About the Author

L. R. Early was born in Saskatoon, Saskatchewan, and received his honors B.A. and M.A. from the University of Saskatchewan, and a Ph.D. in English from York University, Toronto. He has published essays on nineteenth and twentieth-century Canadian literature, and on Commonwealth poetry and fiction. He has held full time teaching positions at the University of North Carolina at Greensboro and Mount Allison University in Sackville, New Brunswick, and is now a member of the Department of English at York University, Toronto.

Preface

Archibald Lampman was a leading member of the Confederation group of writers in late nineteenth-century Canada, and one of Canada's first accomplished poets. But while his poems have attracted continual interest since the 1890s, no book-length critical study has appeared until now. This fact is attributable both to gaps in the information needed for a thorough assessment, and to certain internal problems in Lampman's work. Until recently, most criticism has been based on a limited knowledge of his entire body of writing, and on scanty information about his life and the dates of his poems. Lately, some of these gaps have been filled, making possible a detailed discussion of three major issues: the significance of Lampman's nature poetry, the meaning of his relation to literary tradition, and the measure of unity in his poetic vision. These questions are related, and though at times I emphasize one or another, all three will recur in the chapters that follow.

Lampman's nature poetry has dominated critical attention and provoked very different reactions. Is he a descriptive poet or a myth-making visionary? If both, where is he stronger? And what is the relative importance in his landscape poems of literary tradition, personal sensibility, and the Canadian locale? Such questions may reflect the changing enthusiasms of criticism but they also reflect the variegated character of Lampman's work: more than most writers, he makes us qualify our generalizations. While there is some justice in the preoccupation with his nature poetry, I hope to show that a good deal of his other work also rewards attention.

Throughout this study I stress the importance of Lampman's relation to English Romantic poetry. Some of his more obviously Romantic features have long been noted: his idealism, his melancholy, his keen sense of beauty, and his early death. I propose, however, to work with a more complex idea of Romanticism and a more flexible approach to the problem of influence than some of Lampman's detractors have demonstrated. His essays show that he saw himself as part of a community of writers devoted to refining a vital poetic enterprise, rather than to rejecting or redefining it. At the same time, he was aware that influences can harm the artist who is possessed by them, and he felt such a danger in his own attachment to Keats. We should be careful, then, about dismissing certain poems as merely derivative. Some are that, but others are traditional in the best and most fruitful sense of the word.

The third issue that I address concerns the coherence of Lampman's work. Some early readers, including his friend Duncan Campbell Scott, thought that there was no system whatever to be found in his ideas; indeed, some of Lampman's own remarks on imaginative freedom might encourage that assumption. Recently, a contrary opinion has been advanced by several critics, notably Barrie Davies and D. M. R. Bentley, who have sought to demonstrate the unity and consistency of his vision. My own view, like that of Desmond Pacey and a few other commentators of the 1950s and 1960s, falls between these positions. There are patterns in Lampman's poetry well worth investigating, but there are also irreconcilable contradictions. For a number of reasons, he was unable to sustain the imaginative coherence of his work, which as a whole is more remarkable for its sporadic brilliance than for visionary power.

Because Lampman's work furnishes neither a strict pattern of development nor a strictly consistent vision, I have chosen to focus on his major kinds of poetry, each in its turn. My first chapter is biographical, and my second deals specifically with the issues of influence and coherence. Chapters 3 and 4 are on the nature poetry of the 1880s and early 1890s. Chapter 5, on the "social" poems, and chapter 6, on the love poetry, deal mainly with work of the middle 1890s, and chapter 7 surveys the scattered efforts of the poet's final years. My concluding chapter offers an assessment of Lampman's achievement and of his place in Canadian poetry.

L. R. Early

York University

Acknowledgments

Parts of chapters 2 and 8 have been incorporated in "Archibald Lampman (1861–1899)," in *Canadian Writers and Their Works*, Poetry Series, vol. 2, ed. Robert Lecker, Jack David, and Ellen Quigley. Chapter 6 has appeared as "Lampman's Love Poetry" in *Essays on Canadian Writing*, no. 27 (Winter 1983–84). I am grateful to the librarian of Simon Fraser University for permission to quote from Lampman's letters to Maud Playter, and for providing Lampman's photograph; to the Department of Rare Books and Special Collections, McGill University Libraries, for permission to quote from Lampman's letters to W. D. Lighthall; and to the Public Archives of Canada, the Library of Parliament, and the Thomas Fisher Rare Book Library at the University of Toronto, for access to Lampman's unpublished papers. I wish to thank the Social Sciences and Humanities Research Council of Canada for grants that assisted in the preparation of this study, and the staffs of the Scott Library at York University, the Bell Library at Mount Allison University, and the Simon Fraser University Library, for their courteous assistance. My special appreciation goes to Anne Goddard of the Public Archives, to Joyce Ferguson, who typed the manuscript, and to Gail Donald and Sharon Brooks, who helped with the proofreading.

Abbreviations

ALS   *At the Long Sault and Other New Poems.* Foreword by Duncan Campbell Scott. Introduction by E. K. Brown. Toronto: Ryerson, 1943. Reprinted in *The Poems of Archibald Lampman.* Introduction by Margaret Coulby Whitridge. Toronto: University of Toronto Press, 1974.

CLT   *An Annotated Edition of the Correspondence between Archibald Lampman and Edward William Thomson (1890–1898).* Edited by Helen Lynn. Ottawa: Tecumseh, 1980.

LK   *Lampman's Kate: Late Love Poems of Archibald Lampman, 1887–1897.* Edited by Margaret Coulby Whitridge. Ottawa: Borealis, 1975.

LS   *Lampman's Sonnets 1884–1899.* Edited by Margaret Coulby Whitridge. Ottawa: Borealis, 1976.

MI   *At the Mermaid Inn: Wilfred Campbell, Archibald Lampman, Duncan Campbell Scott in the "Globe" 1892–93.* Introduction by Barrie Davies. Toronto: University of Toronto Press, 1979.

PAL   *The Poems of Archibald Lampman.* Edited by Duncan Campbell Scott. Memorial Edition. Toronto: Morang, 1900. Reprint. *The Poems of Archibald Lampman.* Introduction by Margaret Coulby Whitridge. Toronto: University of Toronto Press, 1974.

SP   *Archibald Lampman: Selected Prose.* Edited by Barrie Davies. Ottawa: Tecumseh, 1975.

Chronology

gland." August: writes "Among the Timothy"; camping trip with D. C. Scott on the Lièvre River.

1887   Writes "The Frogs," May, and "Heat," July. September: marries Maud Playter. Katherine Waddell employed as clerk in the Post Office Department.

1888   Completes "An Athenian Reverie." *Among the Millet* privately published by John Durie and Son, Ottawa.

1890   March: E. W. Thomson's *Globe* editorial on Lampman's behalf; correspondence between Lampman and Thomson begins.

1891   August: visits Thomson in Boston.

1892   11 January: birth of daughter, Natalie. 6 February: "At the Mermaid Inn," column by Lampman, D. C. Scott, and W. W. Campbell, begins to appear Saturdays in the Toronto *Globe*. Lampman writes "The City of the End of Things" and completes "Winter-Store."

1893   Writes "The Character and Poetry of Keats." 24 June: Lampman's final contribution to "At the Mermaid Inn," which terminates the following week.

1894   April: completes "The Story of an Affinity." 12 May: a son, Arnold Gesner, born; dies 4 August.

1895   May: Lampman elected to the Royal Society of Canada. October: writes "Happiness." December: writes "A Vision of April."

1895–1896   Period of crisis involving Katherine Waddell.

1896   After many delays, *Lyrics of Earth* published by Copeland and Day, Boston. Ca. August–September: camping trip with brothers-in-law to the Temiscamingue region.

1897   11 March: death of Lampman's father. June: excursion to Halifax and Amherst, Nova Scotia. September: camping trip with D. C. Scott up the Gatineau River.

1898   February: prostrated by weak heart; given three months leave of absence, later extended to six months. 21 June: son, Archibald Otto, born. July–September: travel and visits in Quebec, Nova Scotia, and Boston.

October: rejoins family in Ottawa, resumes duties at Post Office Department.

1899   29–30 January: writes "Winter Uplands." 8 February: Lampman suffers an attack of acute pneumonia; dies 10 February; buried in Beechwood Cemetery, Ottawa. Twelve copies of *Alcyone* printed by James Ogilvy, Ottawa.

1900   *The Poems of Archibald Lampman,* edited by D. C. Scott, published by George N. Morang and Company, Toronto.

Chapter One

The Clearer Self

"Wherein lies happiness?" Keats's question, cheerfully posed in *Endymion,* became a troubled theme in the life and work of Archibald Lampman. Lampman, who wrote an essay on the subject just at the unhappiest period of his life, looked for an answer in several directions: in an idealized past, in an engagement with present circumstances, and in the prospect of a better day. His concern was never merely selfish, and no doubt he was the more tormented for struggling with the question on behalf of a less generous humanity. At first, like Keats, he believed that happiness lay in the apprehension of beauty and the experience of love. Later, he resorted to reducing expectations and feeding on memory. His story is largely one of disillusionment, hardly an uncommon story, though one of considerable interest when it concerns a poet of Lampman's talent. The contradictions in his life and work reflect the bitter trial and partial dissolution of his personal and poetic faith. The effect upon his career was traumatic, though in the end he found that something peculiarly like happiness might show itself even beyond the anguish of relinquished dreams.

1861–82

Lampman was born on 17 November 1861 in the Anglican rectory near the village of Morpeth, Canada West, on the north shore of Lake Erie. His father, also named Archibald, and his mother, Susanna Gesner Lampman, were both descended from Loyalist families who had fled New York for Canada during the American Revolution. Some of Lampman's forebears fought on the British side in that war, and others were wounded defending Canada in the War of 1812. If, as has been said, "historically, a Canadian is an American who rejects the Revolution," there is something appropriate in Lampman's ancestry.[1] Born into a century of rampant nationalism, he never became a chauvinist, but he did become committed to encouraging a native Canadian literature, and eventually he made a substantial contribution.

In 1866 Lampman's father moved the family to Perrytown, near Port Hope, in what is now east central Ontario. The next year he became rector at Gore's Landing on Rice Lake, and in 1874, curate of St. Peter's in Cobourg. In all these places Lampman lived close to the rolling Ontario landscape re-created so vividly in his poems. His early years at Rice Lake provide a footnote to the continuity of Canadian literature through his acquaintance there with Catharine Parr Traill and Susanna Moodie, two sisters famous for their books on pioneer life. The critical event of his childhood was a severe rheumatic fever in November 1868 that damaged his heart, leaving him lame for four years and ultimately hastening his death at the age of thirty-seven.

Just as a childhood spent close to the countryside fostered Lampman's love of nature, good schools and a talented family nurtured his imagination. In 1870 he entered the school at Gore's Landing conducted by F. W. Barron, an educator noted for his high standards and success. There Lampman acquired basic Greek and Latin, as well as an enduring interest in the classics. From 1874 to 1876 he attended Cobourg Collegiate Institute, then entered the preparatory school for Trinity College, the province's central Anglican institution of higher learning. At this period and later, he had the support and stimulation of his parents and three younger sisters. Reverend Lampman was an enthusiastic reader with a taste for eighteenth-century poetry and intellectual debate. Susanna Lampman was an accomplished organist who played at her husband's services and, on occasion, at Trinity College during her son's years there, after the family moved to Toronto. Belle, the eldest of Lampman's three sisters, provided friendly criticism of his work. Annie, his second sister, eventually studied piano in Germany and became a leader in musical circles in Ottawa. Caroline, nicknamed "Bebe," had a flair for painting and, perhaps encouraged by her brother's example, published a poem in the *Canadian Illustrated News* when she was fourteen. [2]

As a student, Lampman was popular with both teachers and classmates. His biographer, Carl Y. Connor, records that in June 1876 he stood first in several subjects, including the history of Greece and Rome, at Cobourg Collegiate Institute. [3] At Trinity College School, he was head boy and prefect, and in his final year, at the commencement exercises, "he was chaired by his companions and carried in triumph and with much cheering through the buildings and school grounds."[4] For the rest of his life, and to a remarkable degree, Lampman inspired respect and affection in people who came to know him. His warmth and generosity led others to reciprocate, and when his health or finances failed, there were concerned friends to offer support.

In 1879 Lampman passed from the preparatory school in Port Hope to Trinity College in Toronto. He entered as a Foundation Scholar but, as events proved, his social contacts and literary activity were more important to him than his course of study. Fifty years later, a classmate recalled: "In his first term I thought him silent and retiring. That was how he looked; but looks are sometimes misleading. This innocent looking youth burst forth into one of the noisiest students in college and delighted to disturb the quiet of the academic halls after lights were turned off."[5] Lampman's friends at Trinity included John Ritchie, who became an Ottawa crown attorney, Archibald Campbell, who was to be instrumental in finding him a civil service job, and Charles Shortt, one of the recipients of the Christmas poems that Lampman later sent to friends, between 1890 and 1898. Another comrade was Edmund Collins, a Toronto journalist soon to become known for his biography of Sir John A. Macdonald.

Lampman became a member of the Trinity College Literary Institute and an editor and contributor for *Rouge et Noir,* the student magazine. There his first known publication, an essay on Shelley's "Revolt of Islam," appeared in December 1880. His earliest published poem, "Verses," appeared in the February 1882 issue, to be followed by others, especially after his graduation. But most of his student writing for *Rouge et Noir* was prose, including a series of sketches, "College Days among Ourselves," which represent undergraduate life in mellow, wistful tones as a golden time of sheltered freedom and communal affection. These pieces reflect the pleasure that Lampman found in personal relationships and imaginative work. At the same time, his essays on Shelley and Leon Gambetta show the interest in public life, contempt for greed, and commitment to political justice that eventually led him to socialism.

Lampman's writing in *Rouge et Noir* raises the important question of his religious position. His pieces on Shelley and Gambetta qualify his admiration for both men with disapproval of their atheism and their hostility to the Church. Such reservations are not surprising in essays written by a clergyman's son and published in an Anglican college magazine. But by far the greater part of Lampman's work—poems, essays and letters—shows that he came to reject the formal Christianity in which he was raised, though he continued to venerate Christ as an exemplar of "nobility and purity."[6] As his youthful enthusiasm for Shelley suggests, he was acquiring a knowledge of nineteenth-century poetry and contemporary thought that would transform his attitudes. As Barrie Davies has observed, "eventually, for Lampman, Christianity became synonymous with human distress, and was unacceptable because it failed to give men a greater sense of their own potential."[7] Nevertheless, certain values in Lampman's Christian heritage remained rooted in him: selflessness, gentleness, a mistrust of passion, and an abiding sense of the human need for faith. Like so many other nineteenth-century men and women, he abandoned an orthodox creed in the expectation that he would discover a faith more consistent with the advance of knowledge and the facts of contemporary life. Like others, he was to find this problem more difficult than he had imagined.

1882–86

After completing his studies in the spring of 1882, Lampman accepted an appointment at Orangeville High School, northwest of Toronto. He assumed his duties as assistant master on 1 September, returning to Trinity that autumn to write his final examination for the B.A., and passing with second class honors. His experience at Orangeville was progressively unhappy. He wrote to his friend Ritchie, "I teach Latin, Greek, English Literature, History and German. You should hear me lecturing on Scott's 'Marmion' to about thirty big boys, or rather men and girls, most of them a head taller than I am, and able, if they choose, to pitch me out of the window, each one of them with his left hand."[8] His letters both at this time and later indicate that he was frustrated not only by the problem of discipline, but also by his failure to kindle in his students an enthusiasm for literature equal to his own. Moreover, he found little stimulation in his fellow "pedagogues," and discovered that in such circumstances he could do little writing of his own. At Christmas he resigned, and found employment as a temporary clerk in the Post Office Department at Ottawa, an appointment arranged through his Trinity classmate Campbell, the son of Sir Alexander Campbell, then postmaster general of Canada. He took lodgings, and began his new job on 16 January 1883. On 23 March his appointment was made permanent, and he worked there for the remaining sixteen years of his life.

By this time, Lampman was resolved to develop his aptitude for poetry. In the spring of 1881, while still at Trinity, he had come across a book of poems by Charles G. D. Roberts, a young writer from New Brunswick. Its effect upon him was astonishment, and his account of the event, written long afterward, has become a landmark in Canadian literary history:

It was almost ten years ago, and I was very young, an undergraduate at college. One May evening somebody lent me *Orion and Other Poems,* then recently published. Like most of the young fellows about me I had been under the depressing conviction that we were situated hopelessly on the outskirts of civilization, where no art and no literature could be, and that it was useless to expect that anything great could be done by any of our companions, still more useless to expect that we could do it ourselves. I sat up all night reading and re-reading *Orion* in a state of the wildest excitement and when I went to bed I could not sleep. It seemed to me a wonderful thing that such work could be done by a Canadian, by a young man, one of ourselves. It was like a voice from some new paradise of art calling to us to be up and doing.[9]

Lampman's last sentence is charged with a special significance. His notion of a "new paradise of art" has nothing to do with the self-indulgent aestheticism that Tennyson had condemned in "The Palace of Art." On the contrary, it reflects his feeling that in a new country art might have a greater scope to interpret and influence human activity. Despite Lampman's rejection of a conventional creed, the idealism engendered by his education remained the basis of his view of literature.

During 1882 Lampman attempted several kinds of poetry. Most of these efforts are lost or remain in manuscript, although three of them were printed that year in *Rouge et Noir.* The seriousness with which he took his craft is reflected in the fact that he had Edmund Collins, a mutual friend, show some samples to Roberts, and so formed an acquaintance which, though never intimate, brought encouragement. In September 1882 Roberts wrote him a long letter deploring their common lot as school teachers, commenting helpfully on his poems, and advising him against going to British Columbia, a move that Lampman apparently contemplated during his stint at Orangeville. In Ottawa, Lampman's apprenticeship to poetry proceeded more fruitfully. As he informed Ritchie: "I have grown wonderfully prolific of verse since I came here. . . . My verse is continually getting better."[10] In February 1883 the *Canadian Illustrated News* published "Winter Evening," the first of his poems to appear in a vehicle other than *Rouge et Noir*. In December a poem that appears under the title "The Coming of Winter" in *Among the Millet* (1888) was published as "A Monition" in the inaugural issue of the *Week*, a new journal edited by Roberts in Toronto. Although Roberts soon resigned, the *Week* became the leading literary periodical in Canada, and, at its demise in 1896, had published thirty-eight of Lampman's poems, more than had appeared in any other magazine.

From the outset of his writing career, Lampman explored a variety of genres. In 1884 he produced not only love sonnets, nature poems, and miscellaneous lyrics, but also two fairy tales in prose, a romance of some eleven hundred lines in pentameter couplets, entitled "Arnulph," and six chapters of a novel, "the scenes and plot being laid, as I intended, in Granada."[11] These last two projects have never been published, nor have two further verse romances, "Lisa" and "White Margaret," written around 1885. They are thoroughly clichéd love stories, and perhaps reflect Lampman's personal as well as his literary interests at the time. Shorter samples of his early narrative poetry can be seen in "The Organist" (1884) and "The Monk" (1886), both included in *Among the Millet*. Although he abandoned fiction, Lampman continued to write poems of various kinds. In his early years, this eclecticism reflects a desire to find his proper métier, and also, perhaps, the hope that he might make his living as a writer. In his later years, the same eclecticism suggests a determined effort to expand his powers, as well as persistent uncertainty about the nature of his talent. The result was a considerable amount of mediocre work, especially before 1887. But even in this period he produced several splendid pieces, including one of his finest poems, "Among the Timothy" (1885).[12]

There has been a theory that Lampman's situation in Ottawa stifled his creative potential, but most informed comment has stressed the advantages: considerable leisure, interested companions, and ready access to the cultivated countryside and the wilderness beyond.

During the 1880s he appears to have been reasonably content, if sometimes given to the sort of despondency that would reach crisis proportions in the following decade. In December 1884 he wrote to a friend that he had been transferred from the Savings Bank branch of the Post Office Department to the Secretary's Office, and that his less arduous new duties gave him more time for imaginative writing. A few weeks later he wrote to the same friend that he had been "very dull and out of spirits—oppressed with innumerable things—debts; ill success in everything, incapacity to write and want of any hope of ever succeeding in it if I do."[13] This complaint was triggered by the vexation of having some work rejected by the magazines, and by an interval of flagging inspiration. But such moments seem to have been relatively rare. Just as he had made the most of the social and intellectual environment of Trinity College, Lampman entered the intellectual life of Ottawa. In 1884 he heard Matthew Arnold lecture during the latter's North American tour, and the following year delivered a lecture himself, to the Ottawa Literary and Scientific Society, on "The Modern School of Poetry in England." He also joined the Ottawa Social Science Club, Fabian Society, and Audubon Society. His friends were among the city's brightest talents, including the painters William Brymner and Charles Moss, as well as a young clerk in the Department of Indian Affairs, Duncan Campbell Scott.

Eight months Lampman's junior, Scott was also the son of a clergyman, and had also sought a living in the civil service out of necessity rather than preference. Unlike Lampman, Scott rose steadily in his department, and became deputy superintendent general in 1913. In the middle 1880s he was a young bachelor with a taste for the arts, an interest in ideas, and a love of the outdoors. Lampman encouraged his interest in poetry, and in 1887, when both had work coming out in *Scribner's Magazine,* Annie Lampman quoted her brother as saying, perhaps not altogether facetiously, "Duncan and I are marching arm-in-arm to glory."[14] In fact Scott eventually became, with Lampman, one of the three or four outstanding Canadian poets of their generation. After Lampman's death, Scott edited the memorial edition of his friend's poems and also had a hand in two further editions of Lampman's work.

Scott was frequently one of Lampman's companions on his long canoe trips into northern Ontario and Quebec. Another was Ernest Voorhis, who married Belle Lampman, and who recorded some lively

impressions of the poet's delight in exploring remote lakes and
rivers.[15] These camping trips had important consequences in both
Lampman's life and work. "Morning on the Lièvre" (1886) and "The
Loons" (c. 1887) are among his first poems to express an acute sense
of the northern wilderness that gradually came to complement the
more comfortable, settled landscape of his early nature lyrics. Un-
fortunately, the physical effort of these journeys undermined his
health. Scott observed that "for heavy burdens and tasks requiring
great endurance his physique was ill-fitted, yet there was in the
man that robustness of will and tenacity of purpose that prompted
him to lift as if he were a giant and paddle as if he were a trapper."[16]
Later, another friend was to write that Lampman was "physically
brave to an almost reckless degree."[17] Throughout his life, he defied
his chronically fickle health with a relish for strenuous exercise that
was admirable in its bravery but finally tragic in its effects.

During the 1880s Lampman formed one more decisive attachment. In 1884 he met the daughter of a physician who had recently
moved his practice from Toronto to Ottawa. Born in 1867, Maud
Playter was seventeen when she attracted Lampman's notice.[18] Their
letters, written during the absence of one or the other from Ottawa,
provide a good deal of insight into their relationship. His are notable
for their tenderness and lack of all but the most superficial literary
interest. Hers are blithe and filled with chatter about social calls
and shopping excursions. Equally revealing are a number of sonnets
that Lampman wrote during their courtship. Most of these were
published only long afterward, as a sequence titled "The Growth
of Love," in *At the Long Sault and Other New Poems,* a posthumous
selection made from Lampman's manuscripts by Duncan Campbell
Scott and E. K. Brown in 1943. One of these sonnets, composed
in February 1885, clearly illustrates Lampman's romantic idealism,
as well as his debt to Elizabethan models:

> My Lady is not learned in many books
> Nor hath much love for grave discourses, strung
> With gaudy ornament; for she is young
> And full of many pranks and laughing looks;
> And yet her heart hath many tender nooks
> Of fervour and sweet charity; her tongue,
> For all its laughter, yet is often wrung
> With soft compassion for Life's painful crooks.

I love my Lady for her lovely face
And for her mouth and for her eyes and hair;
More still I love her for her laughing grace
And for her wayward ways and changeful air;
But most of all Love gaineth ground apace,
Because my Lady's heart is pure and fair. [19]

While the conventional nature of these lines is patent, they do shed a good deal of light on the young poet and his younger lady. Lampman's view of Maud was very much the old story of illusions struggling with quite evident realities. At one point, while confined for a time with an ulcerated leg, he wrote her a series of letters. In one of these he touchingly affirms his delight in her: "for you are my other self you know, my love." [20] But a few days later he is much less absolute about their affinity, and he refers to the same difference in temperaments acknowledged in his sonnet:

My Darling,

I have received your letter. . . . You recount the many gayeties (I call them "miseries"!) which you have endured—I should say enjoyed—lately. What amuses me, oh strange Little One, is that you commiserate me for having missed all these things. I assure you, Dear, I am heartily thankful I had nothing to do with them. I would much rather be laid up with a sore leg any day. [21]

We should not make too much of a lover's banter. Still, Lampman's letters and sonnets acquire some poignancy in our knowledge that eventually he turned elsewhere for a spiritual mate. In the meantime, about nine months after composing this letter, he married Maud, in September 1887. Their union seems to have been quite normally happy and hopeful for at least half a dozen years, brightened by the poet's aspirations, by mutual affection, and by the birth of a daughter in 1892. Subsequently, the marriage suffered the stresses of a son's death, continuing financial straits, and the illness of both partners. At this later time, another woman became an important presence in Lampman's life, and a crucial one in his imagination.

1887–93

The year 1887 can be taken to mark Lampman's coming of age as a poet. That January he wrote "New Year's Eve" [I], his first

sonnet in almost a year and a half. Before this date he had not
particularly favored the form, having written only five sonnets besides those composed for Maud. Beginning in January 1887, he
produced thirty-nine sonnets in about eighteen months. Some are
of the quality that has led various critics to affirm that Lampman's
essential genius was as a writer of sonnets. Those composed in 1887
include the five sonnet-stanzas of "The Frogs," one of his finest
landscape poems. At this time he also wrote "Heat," the best-known
of all his works, and he finished "An Athenian Reverie," his first
really accomplished long poem. He had hit his stride, entering a
period of creative vigor that lasted for eight years. As the eighties
ended, he was writing regularly and often very well. Sometimes his
sonnets came in bursts, as in the autumn of 1889 when he composed
seven in September and another seven in the last two weeks of
November. His habits of composition have been memorably described by Duncan Campbell Scott:

His poems were principally composed as he walked either to and from his
ordinary employment in the city, upon excursions into the country, or as
he paced about his writing-room. Lines invented under these conditions
would be transferred to manuscript books, and finally after they had been
perfected, would be written out carefully in his clear, strong handwriting
in volumes of a permanent kind.
    Although this was his favorite and natural method of composing, he
frequently wrote his lines as they came to him, and in many of his notebooks can be traced the development of poems through the constant
working of his fine instinct for form and expression: both were refined
until the artist felt his limit. [22]

Lampman's publications did not keep pace with his composition.
Although his work continued to appear in *Rouge et Noir* and the
Week, it was not until late 1887 that he gained a wider audience
with the sale of two sonnets to *Scribner's.* Lampman felt acutely the
lack, at this period, of a sufficient number of Canadian magazines
and publishers to support Canadian writers. Over the next decade,
he was to publish poems in most of the leading American periodicals,
but he continued to have difficulty finding publishers for his books.
In 1888, with a mass of unpublished work on hand, he decided to
issue a volume of poems at his own expense, assisted by a small
legacy that Maud contributed to the cause. *Among the Millet* appeared
toward the end of the year. It was welcomed by Canadian and British

reviewers, and praised by William Dean Howells, the editor of *Harper's,* whose support probably broadened Lampman's access to the American periodical market.

As several critics have observed, some fundamental questions about Lampman's achievement were raised by his earliest reviewers. The first notice of *Among the Millet* appeared in the *Week* for 28 December 1888. Mrs. Frances Harrison, a regular contributor under the nom de plume "Seranus," noted the importance of nature to Lampman and the superiority of his shorter pieces, especially the sonnets. "Fidelis," another pseudonymous reviewer, qualified her praise of *Among the Millet* with the complaint that Lampman's descriptive verse lacked "strong human or subjective interest," a charge echoed by a number of critics in later years.[23] As almost half the pieces in *Among the Millet,* and all in Lampman's second book, *Lyrics of Earth* (1895), are nature poems, it is understandable that the degree of human interest in his verse was something of a crux for his reviewers, though the more acute among them realized that nature poetry may well contain much human, if not specifically social, significance. Most of Lampman's explicitly "social" poems appeared posthumously in *Alcyone* (1899), *The Poems of Archibald Lampman* (1900), and *At the Long Sault* (1943). The ambivalence of early readers about the descriptive lyrics does indicate an important fact about literary taste in the late nineteenth century. Nature poetry had been one of the dominant genres for nearly a century and a half, and by the 1890s many critics were tired of it. "Seranus" pointed out that the changing seasons, Lampman's favorite subject, were "triter than the public know" and "properties the stock in trade of every poet."[24] Similarly, when *Lyrics of Earth* came out, the reviewer for the *Atlantic Monthly* remarked that American verse had been dominated by "lyrists of the woods and fields," and proposed that "perhaps we demand something more than this from our poets."[25] The times were such that Lampman's nature poems, whatever their excellence, encountered an audience that was approaching the point of surfeit with the genre. Perhaps this state of affairs accounts for the paradox of his comparative success in the magazines and difficulty in the book market. Modern readers have been more willing to allow his donnée and accept his nature poetry on its own terms, though there has been some disagreement about what those terms are.

One consequence of the publication of *Among the Millet* was the enlargement of Lampman's circle of friends and admirers. He received complimentary letters from Charles G. D. Roberts, Bliss Carman, Edmund Clarence Stedman, and W. D. Lighthall. The latter, a Montreal lawyer and antiquarian, had edited an important anthology of Canadian verse, *Songs of the Great Dominion* (1889), which included six poems by Lampman. In 1890 the two men exchanged visits, and Lampman was introduced to a circle of writers and artists in Montreal. A still more important acquaintance came about after an editorial "Concerning Archibald Lampman and Sir John Macdonald" appeared in the Toronto *Globe* on 12 March 1890. This editorial urged the prime minister to appoint the author of *Among the Millet* to an easier place in the civil service so that he might have leisure to produce more work of which Canadians could be proud. Lampman sent a letter of thanks to the editorial writer, E. W. Thomson, and a friendship developed that was to be the closest of his later life.

Thomson was a demanding critic, having written to a friend that a great proportion of the verse in Lighthall's anthology was rubbish, although Lampman was "far and away the best poet in the volume— in fact, to me he seems the only cultivated poet—real poet—Canada has ever produced."[26] In 1891 he left the *Globe* for an editorial position with the *Youth's Companion* in Boston. Subsequently that magazine became a regular market for Lampman's poems, and Boston, which he visited several times between 1891 and 1898, another center of interest for him. Thomson became both a sympathetic confidant and a reader whose opinion Lampman respected highly, to the point of consulting him about the content and arrangement of *Lyrics of Earth* in 1895. Their frequent correspondence until a month or two before Lampman's death remains by far the best source of information on the outward events and inner turmoil of the poet's final decade.[27]

Thomson had hardly established himself in Boston before suggesting that Lampman might also find better employment there. His concern was fueled by the latter's complaints about conditions in the civil service and about the difficulty of finding alternative employment in Canada. However, as Helen Lynn has shown, Lampman's character was a greater barrier than adverse circumstance to his advancement.[28] Thomson later noted that his *Globe* editorial might have borne fruit had Lampman been inclined to act: "John

A. thought of giving him something good. But he rather expected Archie to solicit it in some way. The poet was sort of shy, proud— he could not push himself. Sir John died, having done nothing for Lampman" (*CLT,* 2). These remarks are given credibility by Lampman's reaction to several later opportunities. In 1891, during his first visit to Boston, he was introduced to Moses Coit Tyler, a professor of History at Cornell University. Tyler promised to seek a place for him in the English Department at Cornell, but Lampman's initial enthusiasm yielded to misgivings about his fitness for such a post, even before it became clear that Tyler's efforts would prove futile. Again in 1893 Tyler inquired whether Lampman would consider a job in the Cornell Library, and the poet declined, just as he declined Thomson's proposal earlier that year that he come to Boston as a reader for the *Youth's Companion.* In both cases Lampman had reservations about the salary and work, but in both cases also his reluctance seems to have been essentially temperamental. There is no question that Lampman suffered from the nature of his employment in Ottawa, but there can be little doubt that diffidence and lack of material ambition kept him there. The most revealing account of his working environment occurs in a letter of 20 May 1892 to Lighthall:

The Civil Service has some advantages for the literary man, situated as he is in this country with no supporting public; but he needs a great reserve of intellectual vitality to enable him to outlive the routine and monotony of the life. Moreover the political atmosphere which pervades everything in Ottawa is becoming so foul, so utterly sickening, that it is a moral misery and I think a moral damage to any man of high & fine sensibilities to keep himself in contact with it. For my part I intend to get out of it at the very first fairly promising opportunity. Life in Ottawa is a *heavy strain* on a man's patriotism; if I live here much longer I fear I shall become an annexationist.[29]

Lampman did not become an annexationist, nor did he go to the United States when Thomson and Tyler opened up possibilities for his doing so. In the first place, he was constrained by timidity and by concern for his young family. In the second, his work in the civil service did not, despite its repugnant aspects, seriously hamper his writing. The range and quality of his poetry are evidence of this fact, as is a letter to Thomson of 26 October 1894 (*CLT,* 126). Finally, and perhaps most fundamentally, Lampman detested the prevailing ethic in North American life that identifies success with affluence, and he believed that this ethic was likely to warp the vision of writers and artists. From his earliest years, he championed "the poet's sovereign indifference to wealth."[30] While this principle sustained his creative integrity, he suffered its consequence in his limited means and in his anxiety on his family's behalf.

As the 1890s proceeded, Lampman was troubled by this tension and others. His regard for privacy and predilection for dreams ran counter to his conviction that strong poets were the better for taking part directly in public life. Always a Romantic, he felt that poets ought to second their visions with action, but his gestures to that end were limited to his activity in the various clubs to which he belonged, and to his part in "At the Mermaid Inn," a weekly column that appeared in the Toronto *Globe* between 1892 and 1893.

This column was a joint venture by Lampman, Duncan Campbell Scott, and a third Ottawa poet, William Wilfred Campbell, who also worked in the civil service. The title was Scott's idea, inspired by Keats's poem about the celebrated haunt of Shakespeare, Ben Jonson, and other Elizabethan poets. The initial column, with several pieces by each of the contributors, appeared on 6 February 1892. It continued to run on Saturdays until 1 July 1893, when it was brought to an end, apparently by an editorial decision at the *Globe,* but perhaps by a rift between Campbell on one side, and Scott and Lampman on the other.[31] In the interval, Lampman contributed more than one hundred brief essays on literature, national and international events, social issues, painting, wildlife, and other subjects. These pieces show his ability to write graceful prose, and they reveal much about his milieu. They reflect the humor that also appears in his letters, if seldom in his poetry. Amid a great variety of topics, he returns frequently to certain persistent themes. One of these is the tragedy of talent wasted through parental ignorance, the misguided choice of a vocation, or other circumstances. In one column he applauded Canadians who had gone abroad to win honors: "Here their energies might have withered away in petty and fruitless occupations, and their talent have evaporated in the thin sluggishness of a colonial atmosphere" (*MI,* 270). The pertinence of this remark to his own case is obvious, and it foreshadows the frustration that was to ravage him two years later. He observed in another column: "the good man desires to bring himself into the nearest and readiest touch with the universal human soul, and this he can only do by the most complete development and revelation of his own individuality. He must be himself most thoroughly before he can enter with real sympathy into the hearts of others" (*MI*, 23). Soon he would find that the self was a more ambiguous thing, and his idealism would be tested severely by the loss of his sense of self-possession.

In general, though, the early 1890s were busy, hopeful years for Lampman. Besides writing for the *Globe* and occasionally lecturing on literature, he regularly published poems in the periodicals, adding *Harper's* and the *Atlantic Monthly*, among others, to his list. In 1893 his work was given prominence in *Later Canadian Poems*, edited by J. E. Wetherell. In January 1892 his daughter Natalie was born. In October he moved his family to a larger house, and in November 1893 he was promoted to second class clerk, with the "somewhat increased salary" of eleven hundred dollars (*CLT*, 102). His writing during this period was typically diverse. He wrote sonnets on moral themes as well as on the seasons, places, and the weather. His lyrics of middle length include meditative landscape poems, symbolic allegories, and narrative monologues. In 1891–92 he reworked two early long pieces, "Lisa" and "David and Abigail." Nature poems, however, accounted for most of his sales to magazines, and in 1892 he put together a manuscript consisting largely of nature poetry. This volume, tentatively titled "Pictures and Meditations," met with a disheartening series of rejections by various publishers before it was finally issued, in somewhat revised form, as *Lyrics of Earth* in the spring of 1896.

This long delay in the publication of Lampman's second volume has rather obscured the course of his development as a writer. Almost all the poems in *Lyrics of Earth* were written by 1893, and by the time that volume appeared, his interests had shifted significantly. Similarly, most of the poems in his third volume, *Alcyone*, were written by 1895, four years before that book went to press. Nevertheless, something like a consensus about Lampman's poetic career has emerged. As early as 1901, Duncan Campbell Scott noted that while "the first impulse of his genius was the interpretation of nature," it was always accompanied by an interest in human relations: "From the earliest of his writings to the latest this secondary quality demands attention, will be heard, keeps gaining strength and importance."[32] As a generalization about Lampman's development, this statement will do, and has been echoed by many critics.

A fallacy that often attends it, however, interprets the nature poems and "social" poems as somehow discrete, when from the beginning they are complementary. Lampman's sense of human destiny is chiefly expressed in parables and visions of apocalyptic cities, which appear almost as early as the nature lyrics, in such poems as "The Weaver" (1883), "A Fantasy" (1883), and "The Three Pilgrims" (1885). The consummate expression of this vision is "The City of the End of Things," written in the summer of 1892 and first published in the *Atlantic Monthly* for March 1894.

Between February and July 1893, "Pictures and Meditations" was rejected by three publishers. This ill success strengthened Lampman's resolve to do other kinds of work, for by this time he had come to feel that landscape poetry was too limited to encompass his poetic vision. That spring he closed the manuscript book in which he had made fair copies of his poems over the preceding four years, and he began a new one. His writing in the summer and fall of 1893 included one or two nature poems, but was dominated by prophetic lyrics and psychological studies. In October he informed Thomson, "I am going to make up another volume of poems— volume No. 3—before the winter is out—and send it round upon the track of the other one. It will be a different kind of collection— less description, more human life. Perhaps it will take" (*CLT,* 94). He also sent a large sample of his recent work to Thomson, whose response was discouraging. Chagrined, Lampman replied that he appreciated his friend's careful reading of the poems in question, and that he was the more dismayed because he had written them out of what he thought "a genuine impulse":

What is man to do when his apparently genuine impulses betray him? I think I have learned a lesson—the fact viz., that I must stick, like the Shoemaker to my last. There is one kind of work I can do—I know that you always find it satisfactory—nature-work, as they call it—and I had better confine myself to that. To go afield out of my line, I foresee, will only involve me in bitter disappointment and the sense of failure, which is the worst hell that the human soul can know. (*CLT,* 101)

In fact Lampman did not retreat to "nature-work." His confidence was shaken, but he continued to act on his other imaginative impulses, and later he would be readier to defend them. In the meantime, he concentrated on finishing "The Story of an Affinity," the first long poem that he had attempted in years. This "small novel in blank verse" was begun around November 1892 and completed in April 1894. Its theme was romantic love, a subject that he had all but dropped since his courting days, but that now preoccupied him again.

1894–99

The next two years were turbulent ones for Lampman. He was troubled by financial worries, but these were the least of his problems. On 28 February 1894 he wrote to Thomson, "I am becoming morbid, subject to dreadful moods and hypochondria" (*CLT,* 106); and a week later: "I suppose I am passing through some spiritual revolution; in fact I know I am; and some things have caused me unusual agonies" (*CLT,* 107). One cause of his distress was doubt about the value of his writing. Another blow fell when his infant son Arnold, born on 12 May, died after a bout of dysentery, on 4 August. "My little lad's death has given me the horrors," he wrote to Thomson; "this loss has brought upon me what I never experienced before—a thorough disgust of life" (*CLT,* 123, 124). Nevertheless, neither self-doubt nor grief stifled his creative impulse. The spring of 1894 brought a burst of imaginative energy that produced more than a dozen sonnets, six of them within a week; and in late August he wrote four poems for his dead son, including the delicate and moving elegy, "White Pansies."

For two more years, Lampman's moods of despair continued, with some intervals of renewed confidence. His futile efforts to find a publishing house for his books galled him. In addition to "Pictures and Meditations," the nature lyrics that had been in submission to various publishers since 1892, he had made up two other volumes. One, a collection of poems on "human life" assembled in late 1893, was eventually titled "Alcyone." The other, a collection called "A Century of Sonnets," put together in late 1894, he regarded as his best volume. Neither found a publisher, and he chafed at their failure. On 29 August 1895, he defended some recent work against Thomson's criticism, and declared his intention to leave the civil service in about four years. At that time he hoped to be superannuated: "I shall go to some small quiet country place and give myself up to poetry. I can make a few hundred a year by the pen, and there is no reason why I should not be comfortable, and above all—*free*. It is freedom that I want. I am bound. I am suffocated. If I had the genius of Milton I could do nothing" (*CLT*, 150).

Lampman's unhappiness at this time was compounded by a domestic crisis hinted at here and there in the correspondence with Thomson, especially in his letters of 30 September 1895 and 11 February 1896. Maud's health had collapsed after their son's death, and remained poor for the next two years. Like Lampman, who was himself often ill with influenza, she suffered from a weak heart. Recent studies of Lampman by Bruce Nesbitt and Margaret Coulby Whitridge have emphasized the vicissitudes in his marriage, and his friendship with a woman named Katherine Waddell during the 1890s.[33] Speculation about his relations with "Kate," especially about the nature of their intimacy and its duration, should be treated cautiously, but the evidence does suggest that for two years, at least, culminating in a crisis during the winter of 1896, Lampman was passionately attracted to her, and that consequently his writing suffered.

Katherine was a year and a half older than Maud, and worked in Lampman's department of the civil service. Whitridge claims that Lampman fell in love with her in 1889, while Nesbitt suggests that it was not until 1892. Both suppose that it was in 1893 that Lampman presented her with his recently completed manuscript volume, containing fair copies of his work dating from about 1888 to February 1893. The curious thing about this gift is that it includes almost no love poetry, and that the sonnet placed last, bearing the significantly domestic title "Angela Domi," praises "my lady of the brave blue eyes"—that is, Maud, for Katherine was grey-eyed, as several of Lampman's poems about her indicate. This sign of fidelity to his wife indicates that as late as the early part of 1893, Lampman still regarded Katherine simply as a friend, no doubt one who had shown an interest in his poetry. The development of stronger feelings probably dates from September or October of that year, when he wrote the first lyrics that can be taken to reflect his attraction to her: "Personality" (*PAL*, 185), "Fate" (*ALS*, 24), and "I May Not Love You."[34] These are very likely the poems that he refers to in a letter to Thomson of 6 November, which addresses the question of an autobiographical element in his work (*CLT*, 97).

Whitridge and Nesbitt both think that Lampman did come to love Katherine Waddell profoundly, and that she ultimately rejected his attentions, probably around 1895–96, precisely that period at which his letters reveal a depth of anguish that can be explained only in part by his depression over the state of his writing.[35] Certain poems that Lampman wrote at this time support this inference. Some are reminiscent of the love poetry written during his courtship. Just as he had composed sonnets in the Elizabethan manner for Maud, so he returned to that model in a number of sonnets for Katherine. Scott, who was to arrange the earlier sonnets as "The Growth of Love," would also group six of the later ones under the title "A Portrait in Six Sonnets," in *At the Long Sault*. The following, dated 28 July 1896, is typical. While its conventional likeness to the sonnets in "The Growth of Love" is obvious, it also presents certain suggestive contrasts:

> Light-footed and light-handed, quick to feel,
> And sensitive as water—life to her
> Its sweetest and its bitterest shall reveal,
> Yet leave her a secure philosopher.
> The spirit's inward hunger and thought's care,
> Strange birthgift of our dark witch mother, Truth,
> Have only given her what is tenfold fair,
> The grace of knowledge with the grace of youth.
> Impulsive, yet clear-minded, nature's stress
> Keeps her too human for the stoic's part,
> And wisdom hath she for her lord no less,
> A wary helmsman to the generous heart.
> Her friendship—'tis for them to know the worth
> Of all things subtlest and most rare on earth.
>
> (ALS, 43)

Here it is intelligence and moral beauty, not kisses and girlish caprice, that compel the poet's interest. This contrast with the sonnets for Maud is probably as good a clue as any to the qualities that attracted Lampman to Katherine. In the "Six Sonnets" she is never "My Lady" but, repeatedly, a "friend" whose intellectual quickness and sympathy draw the poet's admiration. The six sonnets selected by Scott are noticeably chaste in sentiment, and certainly much less sensuous than those in "The Growth of Love." Still, they do not tell the whole story. Between 1893 and 1897 Lampman wrote more than two dozen other lyrics that probably reflect his relationship with Katherine. Most of these have been published only recently, in *Lampman's Kate* (1975). Many express intense feelings that Scott excluded from his more limited selection, and a number refer bitterly to the fate that prevents the poet and his "friend" from acting upon their feelings. Perhaps it is no coincidence that, having twice failed to find an enduring joy in love, Lampman completed an essay in the autumn of 1895 that recommends sublimation, acceptance, and memory as the only firm basis for happiness.[36]

Lampman apparently took little pleasure in his election to the Royal Society of Canada in May 1895. Also, his satisfaction at having *Lyrics of Earth* accepted by Copeland and Day diminished steadily as a series of problems delayed its publication. When it finally appeared in the spring of 1896, it was favorably reviewed but, as Lampman wrote to Thomson, "did not sell" (*CLT,* 192). Meanwhile, his creative efforts were scattered. "The Story of an Affinity" shows that an idealized conception of love had become crucial to his imagination; the bitter personal experience that followed brought a hiatus in his development as a poet. He continued to produce some very good poems, but his sense of purpose and direction was gone. His later work shows some recovery from this emotional and imaginative debacle, but cannot be called an advance, despite some excellent sonnets and several fine longer poems, including "The Minstrel" (1896) and "At the Long Sault" (1898).

In July 1896 Lampman submitted his "Alcyone" collection to Copeland and Day, who kept him in doubt about their intentions for nearly a year and a half. On 2 November 1897 he informed Thomson: "Copeland & Day having backed out of publishing for me this autumn, I am thinking of going into the publishing business again myself. I can sell enough copies in 6 months to pay the cost and then, if anything comes in, it is mine. Besides I shall not feel myself under obligation to a publisher who is losing on my account. I shall get my book printed and bound in Edinburgh . . ." (*CLT,* 195). Lampman proceeded with this plan, and before the end of 1898 he had the proofs of *Alcyone* in hand. Gradually, he also emerged from his deep unhappiness. In the autumn of 1896 he took an extended camping trip to the Temiscamingue region of northern Ontario. According to Scott, it was probably on this journey that he badly strained his heart. If so, his continued indulgence in hard exercise must have sealed his fate. On 26 July 1897 he reported casually in a letter to Thomson: "I am somewhat sore bodily this morning. I rode a bicycle yesterday morning, and going down a steep place at a good speed got pitched over an embankment head first—byke and all—into a mass of raspberry briars. After that I paddled ten miles and portaged the canoe on my sole shoulders a couple of times, besides doing various other scrambling and hawling. As I said I am sore, but have a good conscience" (*CLT,* 188). In September he made yet another canoe trip, with Scott, up the Gatineau River north of Ottawa. Whatever physical toll these ventures took, they also inspired some of the best poems of his last years, notably the wilderness sonnets of November 1896, and "The Lake in the Forest," probably written in the autumn of 1897.

Lampman's marriage also recovered some of its earlier contentment. On 21 June 1898, Maud gave birth to a son, Archibald Otto, the subject of the sonnet "Last Child."[37] But by then Lampman was seriously ill. In February he had suffered a severe exhaustion that kept him in bed for several weeks and rendered him incapable of exerting himself without pain. His physicians explained that for years his vigorous activity had aggravated the heart condition that dated back to his childhood. Lampman's letters to Thomson report these facts cheerfully, without a hint of self-pity. Indeed, his correspondence in the final year of his life expresses a recovered calmness and geniality that had been absent from his writing for some time.

Lampman took six months' leave from his job and by July 1898 had recovered strength enough to travel through eastern Canada and New England, visiting friends and seeing parts of the country that were new to him. In Montreal he stayed with William Henry Drummond, author of *The Habitant and Other French Canadian Poems.* Another young poet, Arthur Stringer, has left a memorable picture of his meeting with Lampman at Drummond's home. Stringer was profoundly impressed by Lampman's quiet inner strength and devotion to poetry: "He did not carry the torch it seemed to me: he was the torch itself."[38]

In October 1898, having seen Thomson in Boston, Lampman wrote from Ottawa that he had arrived safely back, and had returned to work: "I found my little family very glad to see me. My wife is fairly well, but she has had a rather hard summer. I must make it up to her another year" (*CLT,* 210). This last remark is sad in its unintended irony. A few months later, on 8 February 1899, Lampman suffered an attack of acute pneumonia. He died on 10 February at about one in the morning, and was buried the next day in Ottawa's Beechwood Cemetery. *Alcyone,* the book that he had planned and revised since 1893, was in press at the time. As his literary executor,

Scott limited the printing to twelve copies and set about editing the larger memorial edition of his work. *The Poems of Archibald Lampman* was advertised as a subscription to raise money for the author's family, and was published in 1900 by Morang and Company of Toronto. An ample, attractive book, it incorporated *Among the Millet, Lyrics of Earth,* and *Alcyone,* and added over one hundred more poems. It was immediately successful and soon went into further printings, confirming Lampman's importance as the key figure among the Canadian poets of his generation.

Chapter Two
Lampman's Troubled Dreams

The Romantic Heritage

"A good deal is being said," Lampman remarked in 1891, "as to whether a Canadian literature exists. Of course it does not."[1] In the ensuing passage of his essay "Two Canadian Poets," he recounted his joy ten years earlier at discovering Roberts's *Orion*. As many readers have realized, Lampman's anecdote provides an ideal starting point from which to consider the Confederation poets of his generation, and their place in Canadian literature. Clearly, Lampman felt that he was in a literary void and was deeply interested in the prospects for Canadian poetry, though he attached more importance to its literary merit than to its Canadian content. *Orion,* after all, draws heavily on the English Romantics and Victorians, and Roberts himself later dismissed it (too harshly) as "derivative stuff."[2]

Lampman's essay shows him to be a moderate nationalist, more concerned with supplying his country's deficiencies than with proclaiming its virtues. His "At the Mermaid Inn" columns similarly protest "the arid poverty of our social and intellectual life" and complain of the meager opportunity for talent in Canada.[3] As a literary critic, he foreshadows the view taken some fifty years later by such writers as E. K. Brown and John Sutherland that the proper approach to Canadian poetry is "a self-critical Canadianism": an appreciation of its individuality combined with a judgment informed by the highest standards.[4] While he was convinced of the importance of a distinctive Canadian literature, Lampman was equally convinced of the importance of the great literature of every time and place to Canadian writers and readers alike. Twice he argued in "At the Mermaid Inn" that "the foundation of a national structure in art" required a publicly supported gallery that would collect the best in both foreign and Canadian art; and he noted that "there is no education for the artist apart from nature, whether in painting, music, literature, or any other like the contemplation of a great and inspiring model (*MI,* 24 June 1893, 337).[5]

In appraising the contribution of the Confederation poets, the question of models is paramount. A great deal of their poetry challenges our ability to discriminate superficial imitation from a creative use of tradition: both responses appear throughout their work, often within the bounds of a single poem. It could hardly be otherwise for writers who combined a profound respect for English and European traditions with the desire to create a new literary world in their transatlantic home. Their poetry was not shaped, as some have argued, by an undue deference to their public, but rather by a high regard for the great writers of the past. Lampman and his contemporaries shared a respect for tradition that runs counter to the iconoclastic aesthetics of our own century. They modified Romanticism's radical emphasis upon original genius with a devotion to the Romantics themselves that (paradoxically) approaches literary conservatism. The question is how far their work is enhanced, and how far damaged by such attitudes.

The issue is as complex as the variety of style and temper among the Confederation poets themselves. Although Roberts wrote to Lampman in 1888 that together with Bliss Carman they would "make this a glorious epoch in our country's history," there was no uniform aesthetic viewpoint among members of the group.[6] They disagreed strongly over the relative merits of the English Romantics, with Lampman and Duncan Campbell Scott as partisans of Wordsworth, and Roberts and Wilfred Campbell insisting on Shelley's superiority.[7] Furthermore, they were open to a range of other influences as their careers developed and assumed individual shapes. Here a salient fact is simply that Lampman's contemporaries survived him by decades. Partly for this reason, his poetry remained closest to its Romantic roots; hence it is in his work that we can see most clearly the value that English Romantic poetry had for the pioneers of a Canadian tradition.

The most obvious use that the Confederation writers made of their Romantic heritage is in their nature poems. Canadians seem always to have felt strongly the need to situate their imaginations, and when the Dominion was formed in 1867 this need acquired special force. The Confederation group found in Romantic poetry splendid demonstrations of how to manage the transactions of mind with landscape. Wordsworth's transfigurations of the ordinary encouraged them to seek the imaginative potential in their own surroundings, as, for instance, the Maritime poets Roberts and Carman memorably did in *Songs of the Common Day* (1893) and *Low Tide on Grand Pré* (1893). The Romantic transformation of Christian values also had a powerful attraction for young men who were reacting, however timorously, against the religious orthodoxy of their own times and fathers. Moreover, the emphasis in Romantic literature on self-discovery and growth complemented the desire among the Canadian poets to produce a new national literature. In 1888 Roberts noted that "out of what is called Romanticism has arisen the most stimulative poetry"; and looking back on the Confederation group some forty years later, he wrote: "in the deep but more or less unconscious optimism of a new country whose vision is fixed upon the future, they had no time for the pessimism and disillusionment of the old world."[8] In addition, the technical virtuosity of Romantic poetry offered its heirs not only a great variety of models, but also a pattern of experimentation and diversification.

Lampman's work comprehends all these aspects of Romantic poetry. More particularly, Keats influenced much of his youthful work, especially the pastoral character of his early landscapes and his idealization of sexual love. The English poet's ode "To Autumn" seized Lampman's imagination as nothing else ever did, and conditioned his own seasons lyrics with their rich texture and elusive patron spirits. While he produced many lovely poems in this mode, most readers would probably agree that they tire by repetition and that (as Lampman himself sensed) in this phase of his work an initial stimulation became an unfortunate enchantment. More essentially, Lampman adopted from Keats the idea of a "dream" wherein the individual can transcend time and strife. This is the key idea in Lampman's writing but it was subverted by experience, meditation, and its tendency to isolate him from other human beings. Ultimately he was led to a renunciation of youthful dreams that parallels Keats's own development.

Although his friend Scott claimed that "Keats was the only poet whose method he carefully studied," clearly Lampman learned as much from Wordsworth.[9] If he found in Keats a model of sensuous gratification in the beauty and melody of nature, he discovered in Wordsworth a method by which to interpret his mind's workings in terms of natural imagery. Wordsworth's poetry honed Lampman's appreciation of the common, unimposing things in nature, and strengthened his resistance to the fake sublimity of so much pseudo-Romantic poetry. No doubt it was Wordsworth too, who fostered his belief in the healing virtue and redemptive power of nature, though here again Lampman came to modify his faith in a way that recapitulates a pattern implicit in his Romantic precursor.

Shelley's influence on Lampman is less palpable. He was almost as powerful a presence in Lampman's imagination as Keats and Wordsworth, but a presence that Lampman resisted, and perhaps not only for the reasons given in his prose. We know that Lampman changed his early enthusiasm—perhaps based on partial or superficial reading—for a highly critical view of Shelley's lack of "the human," egotism, and "fantastic imagination."[10] It is likely, however, that this censure of a former favorite had a deeper cause. As the poet of "Alastor," "Adonais," and "The Triumph of Life," Shelley is the most anti-Romantic of the great Romantics, the most prone to pessimism and despair, and Lampman probably saw this tendency within himself, and recoiled from it. More particularly, he would be made uneasy by Shelley's ultimately bleak view of nature, visions of life as a fevered dream, and inclination to embrace death.

What Lampman admired in the Romantics was as much moral as it was aesthetic. Against the darker moments in Shelley's work— and in his own—he affirmed that great poetry strengthens the understanding and the spirit, and he approved Keats's view that it should "relieve the sordid gloom of human existence."[11] His clearest statement of this position appears in one of his earliest essays, "The Modern School of Poetry in England" (1885):

It seems to me . . . that there is one thing concerning the true life which may be laid down as a guide in criticism. It is this: life is not a dreary thing. Human beings are not mere hopeless playthings in the hands of chance,—governed by a multitude of passions, that must mar and twist them, befoul them or beautify them as they will. Human nature may be represented by the ancient Pan—half human and half beast—but the human is the mightier part, and the whole is ever striving to be divine. The main current of the human spirit, through many changes and many falls, is setting eternally toward a condition of order, and divine beauty and peace. A poet may never have uttered this thought, may never perhaps have been even conscious of it, but unless the general body of his work is in some way accordant with it, unless his transfiguration of life has in some way tended to strengthen and glorify the universal yearning for order and beauty and peace, the heart of man will keep no hold of it.[12]

Here we can see both Lampman's similarity to the Romantics and certain significant differences. He is at one with them in regarding poetry's true purpose as serving the advance of the human spirit toward an ultimate renovation and transfiguration. The English Romantics, however, generally valued passion as an aspect of imaginative strength, and they tended to stress the process rather than the final issue of our destiny. Lampman's didactic account of Pan recalls the long decades of Victorian gravity that succeeded Keats's and Shelley's ecstatic evocations of myth. His strictures on the irrational side of human nature and his vision of an ideal state of ordered peace express not universal values, but personal or cultural attitudes, a deep mistrust of passion and a longing for repose that, in the extreme, became a hankering after death. There may be a trace of the latter feeling even in his language here, in the implied metaphors of sunset and rivers-to-the-sea.

Although Lampman's conception of great art as spiritual enlightenment is seldom expressed as reductive moralizing, at times he did invoke social values against poetry of which he disapproved. He censured Byron, for example, as "a disturbing influence to human progress," and he was explicit in declaring that "art is a non-moral thing, and may be good or bad, according to the nature of him who uses it."[13] Generally, though, he thought of poetry as being opposed to the diseased order of a materialistic society. His standards are indicated in a column contributed to "At the Mermaid Inn" on 7 January 1893, where the familiar exercise of choosing half a dozen books for sojourn on a desert island yields a supreme tradition comprising the Bible, the works of Homer, Shakespeare, and Wordsworth, *Don Quixote,* and Goethe's autobiography: "From these six books a man might draw sufficient strength, knowledge, inspiration, delight, and humanity to last him a lifetime, and leave him with a soul fitted for eternity with all its chambers draped and furnished and all its windows open" (*MI,* 231). Lampman's metaphor combines two famous passages in Keats's letters on human life as a series of chambers in a mansion and on the world as a "vale of Soul-making"; perhaps this implies honorable mention among the truly great for Keats, whom Lampman ranked second only to Wordsworth among the poets of his own century.[14]

Lampman considered the Romantic movement to be the latest flowering of this tradition, and the Romantic poets to have inaugurated a "spiritual awakening, such as had not been known since

the days of Elizabeth."[15] In his "At the Mermaid Inn" column of
8 April 1893, he affirms "a new conception of the higher life" that
is essentially Romantic in outlook:

This conception is the child of science, reinforced by the poetry that is
inherent in the facts of the universe and all existence. Thus reinforced,
the conception is a religious one. It is independent of the ancient creeds,
for it does not trust for its effects to any system of post-mortem rewards
and punishments. It is different from the old stoic virtue of the philosophers, which at bottom was merely prudence, a utilitarian quality. This
modern conception is not a materialistic one, although at first it may seem
so; it is, as I have said, poetic and intrinsically religious. It comes to those
whom the new knowledge has made acquainted with the vast facts and
secrets of life, arming them with a breadth and majesty of vision which
withers away from the soul the greeds and lusts and meannesses of the
old, narrow, and ignorant humanity. The small ambitions and petty passions of this world seem infinitesimal indeed to him who once enters into
the new conception and lives, as it were, in the very presence of eternity.
As yet this new spiritual force only acts upon the few, for it is a modern
thing, but its growth is sure. Spreading downward, with the steady extension and dissemination of culture, from mass to mass, it may in the
end work its way into the mental character and spiritual habit of all
mankind. Then, indeed, the world will become less and less a hospital,
and the old cankerous maladies gradually decline and disappear. (*MI*, 291)

Lampman, like most of his Romantic precursors—and unlike some
of his Victorian contemporaries—saw science and poetry as coop-
erative modes of knowledge. More significantly, he shared their
concern for salvaging values from what he believed to be an obsolete
religious system and for adapting these values to a human, rather
than a supernatural, dispensation. While his identification of poetic
with religious faith is reminiscent of Arnold in "The Study of Poetry," it also harks back to the major English poets at the opening
of the nineteenth century. Like Blake, Shelley, and Wordsworth,
he envisages an ultimate transformation in the human condition
brought about through this "new conception," and he regards the
great poetry of all ages as its agent, if not its source. His devotion
to Romantic values is also clear in his antipathy to the post-Romantic
movements of his own time: "the dreary and monotonous realism
of almost all our present literature," and the "morbid unhealthiness
of the soul" that he saw in the Pre-Raphaelites.[16]

The tradition of prophetic humanism was fertile ground for Lampman's sense of identity as a poet, and the more important to him in the absence of a distinctively national tradition. His work does, however, differ from that of Blake, Wordsworth, Shelley, and Keats in one very important way. While he was devoted to his art, he lacked their drive towards an ultimate synthesis. The sheer variety of influences and attitudes in his poetry indicates an uncertain and eclectic disposition. And while he turned his affinities with Wordsworth and Keats to good account, he was also subject to less auspicious influences. He was impressed, for instance, by the weaker sides of Tennyson and Arnold—by Tennyson's penchant for abstract conjecture and by Arnold's Stoic streak. Moreover, Lampman's poetic career cannot be described simply in terms of a development from apprenticeship to maturity. Even in his prime, he continued to produce derivative work such as "The Land of Pallas" (1891), a versified reduction of William Morris's *News from Nowhere.* In some cases, the influences on Lampman seem hardly reconcilable. The explanation, of course, is that they corresponded to diverse impulses within him. On the one hand, his use of conventional forms tends to mask a personal and highly temperamental element in his writing. On the other, some of the central conflicts of the nineteenth century are played out again in his poetry.

A Fissured Vision

Lampman outlined his poetic creed in the most considerable body of criticism left by any of Canada's nineteenth-century writers. Most of his discussions were designed as lectures and are graceful and lucid, if loosely structured. His attitudes are typical of his time: a low opinion of the eighteenth century ("the sententious age"); a deep affinity with the Romantics; an insistence on the spiritual dimension of poetry, based upon a belief in the unity of truth and beauty; and a concern with poetry as an expression of character. [17] His criticism is largely impressionistic; indeed, he thought that just as a subject should awaken an "answering harmony" in the poet's soul, so should the poem affect the reader. [18] He also believed that the poet's reach should exceed his grasp, for "to aim at the highest level, with a partial failure, is greater than to attain to an absolute perfection in a lower one." [19] Accordingly, in "Two Canadian Poets," he prefers George Frederick Cameron's spontaneity and "truth" to Charles G. D. Roberts's low-pulsed craftsman's hand.

By the late nineteenth century, Lampman could absorb such principles directly from the literary atmosphere. His lectures and essays are not, however, an altogether reliable guide to his performance as a poet. Whereas his criticism suggests a confident mind in command of a stable sense of identity, a general understanding of history, and a considered theory of poetry, his poems and letters show quite another personality: full of ambivalence, and compelled by mood rather than disciplined by thought. Of the many tensions in his work, probably the most painful for him was the erosion of his Romantic faith in the power of poetry by a suspicion that it may, after all, be of little consequence in the scheme of things.

Lampman's uncertainties are more evident in poems that express his self-consciousness as a writer than in his prose criticism. While some of these celebrate the glory of art and the artist's heroic strength, others express reservations about the ultimate importance of poetry and reflect the anguish of the poet's vocation. In the first group, perhaps the most emphatic affirmation occurs in "The Poet's Song" (1890), which depicts an archetypal bard whose vision will redeem his society. Several earlier poems also declare the poet's self-sufficiency as a privileged soul sustained by his vision against the demands of the world and the calamities of experience. However, the very titles of two of these—"Why Do Ye Call the Poet Lonely?" (1884) and "What Do Poets Want with Gold?" (1884)—convey the bravado that undermines their claims. "To the Prophetic Soul" (1893) is similarly unconvincing in its assertion of the poet's autonomy. Whereas Wordsworth had invoked the "prophetic Spirit" (in his prospectus to "The Recluse") to foster his vision as a "benignant influence" in the troubled world, Lampman seizes upon the phrase to express a revulsion from worldly involvement and scorn of the common lot of men:

> Nay, for they are not of thy kind,
>   But in a rarer clay
> God dowered thee with an alien mind;
>   Thou canst not be as they.
>
>
> Be strong, therefore; resume thy load
>   And forward stone by stone

> Go singing, though the glorious road
> Thou travellest alone.
>
> (*PAL*, 201)

Much of Lampman's work suggests that this stance is insupportable. In "The Weaver" (1883) and "The Organist" (1884), he depicts artists whose visions are tragically incommensurate with life. The former is especially notable for its account of the weaver's vision as a "gray" dream of a "dim shadowy land" (*PAL*, 57, 58): the twilit realm of passive serenity, which becomes a recurring fantasy in Lampman's work.[20] The latter poem illustrates a conflict between the artist's vocation and his need of love, a problem that is central to "An Athenian Reverie" (c. 1885–88) and that was strongly felt in Lampman's life. A number of lyrics also express the frustration that attends poetic vision. "Song" (1886) ponders the "Sweet mights that make us sing, / But bring no resting to us" (*PAL*, 41); "Music" (1887) evokes ". . . gleams / Of what we would, and what we cannot be" (*PAL*, 109); and an unpublished piece, "The Poet" (1893), claims that the poet's insights are achieved only at great personal cost: "His heart is trembling and broken / With the passion he paints so well."[21] In "The Minstrel" (1896), one of Lampman's bleakest and most beautiful poems, the archetypal bard reappears as an utterly alien and ephemeral figure. And in two very late lyrics, "Last Child" (1898) and "Even beyond Music" (1899), Lampman reiterates his sense of an abiding gulf between the shadowy ideals envisaged in art and the world of experience.

Lampman's uncertainties also extend to poems that present an overview of the human condition; and here again, a gulf opens between the prophetic humanism of his Romantic inheritance and the despair that lurked on its borders. "Alcyone," written in 1893 and chosen as the title poem of his last volume, presents an exultant vision of human destiny. It develops in dialectical fashion an essentially Romantic view of the universe, history, and humanity and demonstrates Lampman's belief that in the "new conception of the higher life" there need be no discord between science, poetry, and the religious impulse. Alcyone is the brightest star—"the first of seven"—in the Pleiades constellation. The first half of the poem blends an understanding informed by astronomy with undiminished wonder at the vastness of space and the time taken by starlight to reach a perceiver on earth. It also presents the modern view of the universe as void, which displaced the Christian vision of a celestial firmament imbued with spiritual presence, the abode of God and the heavenly host. (In Lampman's vision of a realm subject to "the power of night," there is, surely, an allusion to Milton's cosmos.) Significantly, there is no anxiety in the speaker's tone, rather an awe that verges on exhilaration. The midpoint of the poem hails the human race as a vital antithesis to the cosmic thesis of silence, dust, and darkness:

> Man! when thou dost think of this,
> And what our earth and its existence is,
> The half-blind toils since life began,
> The little aims, the little span,
> With what passion and what pride,
> And what hunger fierce and wide,
> Thou dost break beyond it all.
>
> (*PAL,* 178)

Far from terrifying, the vision of a limitless universe stimulates in human beings a sense of infinite possibility. And this aspiration is fueled by forces—passion and pride—that the displaced theological dispensation had considered sinful. The first direction that this impulse takes is an exploration of inner space, a descent into the "abyss of mind" that will find within the human spirit "a shelter and a peace majestical"—the security that had previously been sought in God. This vision of interior vistas is followed, however, by a synthesis of expansive terms that appropriate cosmic space as the only measure of human possibility. The closing lines of the poem make an inference from this argument, on behalf of humanity. The "sublime" presence in outer space is to be internalized as a symbol and an inspiration.

"Alcyone" is a better poem than John Sutherland assumed when he denounced its technical debt to Edgar Allan Poe.[22] But, in its celebration of pride and passion, it represents a momentary enthusiasm rather than an abiding conviction on Lampman's part. In a number of other poems that interpret the heavens as clues to human destiny, he finds meanings quite contrary to the affirmations of "Alcyone." In "Night" (c. 1889), the darkness with its "wheeling multitude of stars" (*PAL,* 263) reveals to him the pettiness of his passions and the vanity of "infinite" dreams. In "A Midnight Landscape" (c. 1890), the red star Antares presides, in his mind's eye, over a world of evil triumphant. And in "To Chaucer" (1894), he ponders with Arnoldian melancholy the loss of faith in a benign God and the passing of the medieval regard for limits:

> 'Twas high mid-spring, when thou wert here on earth,
> Chaucer, and the new world was just begun;
> For thee 'twas pastime and immortal mirth
> To work and dream beneath the pleasant sun,
> Full glorious were the hearty ways of man,
> And God above was great and wise and good,
> Thy soul sufficient for its earthly span,
> Thy body brave and full of dancing blood.
> Such was thy faith, O master! We believe
> Neither in God, humanity, nor self;
> Even the votaries of place and pelf
> Pass by firm-footed, while we build and weave
> With doubt and restless care. Too well we see
> The drop of life lost in eternity.
>
> (*PAL*, 271)

The course of intellectual history is envisaged here as an attenuation of life rather than an advance toward freedom. Whatever the warrant of this measured sadness, or of the more spirited rhythms of "Alcyone," these poems illustrate a broad vacillation in Lampman's interpretation of humanity's past, present, and future. Such incongruities recur throughout *The Poems of Archibald Lampman,* in nature lyrics, meditations on the human prospect, and love poems.

Lampman's landscape poetry and his meliorist visions disclose one of the deepest rifts in his imagination: on the one hand, a strong attachment to an Arcadian vision of nature; on the other, a commitment to late nineteenth-century evolutionary idealism. The one is fundamentally emotional and retrospective, the other intellectual and progressive. Lampman adopts Wordsworth's faith in a communion with nature as the remedy for our malaise, but he gives the theme a distinctive emphasis. Wordsworth urges that we turn to nature for our health, and if "return" is sometimes implicit in this counsel, it remains very muted indeed. Lampman's treatment of the theme is more overtly primitivist. He not only calls for us to share in the invigorating strength and beauty of the countryside but also conceives of it as the recovery of a lost mode of experience, a return to Arcadia, to the gods, to the Golden Age of pastoral myth. In "Favorites of Pan" (1892), he fancies that the frogs that pipe in springtime are heirs of the vanished pagan god: their song inspires in a sensitive listener "the same unnamed delight" that Pan once inspired in the people of Arcadia (PAL, 132).

The idea that Christian monotheism estranged humanity from the spiritual bounty of natural beauty occurs also in "Man and Nature" (c. 1890). The assumptions of Arcadianism are that primitive humanity enjoyed a harmony with the natural creation that has been lost, and that the human spirit has since suffered deterioration. Although Lampman resists this logic elsewhere, it remains implicit in much of his nature poetry and is openly expressed in "Freedom" (1887), where he calls men "degenerate children" of earth (PAL, 19).

The idea behind his meliorist poems is precisely contrary: namely, that humanity is evolving away from a base origin toward spiritual perfection. Such poems as "The Better Day" (1890) and "The Largest Life" (1894–97) reflect Lampman's Victorian milieu of discursive speculation and intellectual debate, rather than his Romantic sympathies, and in theme and idiom they obviously derive from Tennyson. "The Clearer Self" (1894) is typical:

> Before me grew the human soul,
>   And after I am dead and gone,
> Through grades of effort and control
>   The marvellous work shall still go on.
>
> Each mortal in his little span
>   Hath only lived, if he have shown
> What greatness there can be in man
>   Above the measured and the known;
>
> How through the ancient layers of night,
>   In gradual victory secure,
> Grows ever with increasing light
>   The Energy serene and pure:
>
> The Soul that from a monstrous past,
>   From age to age, from hour to hour,
> Feels upward to some height at last
>   Of unimagined grace and power.

> Though yet the sacred fire be dull,
>   In folds of thwarting matter furled,
> Ere death be nigh, while life is full,
>   O Master Spirit of the world,
>
> Grant me to know, to seek, to find,
>   In some small measure though it be,
> Emerging from the waste and blind,
>   The clearer self, the grander me!
>   (*PAL,* 199–200)

The Energy, or Soul, would seem to be the collective refinement of the race through history to the present; the individual's life has meaning in so far as he apprehends this achievement and contributes to its advance. "The Clearer Self" differs from "Alcyone" in specifying effort and control, rather than pride and passion, as agents of human aspiration, and it envisages a conquest of darkness by light rather than a union of contraries. The concept here of "a monstrous past" flatly contradicts the Arcadianism of such poems as "Favorites of Pan," resembling, rather, Tennyson's vision of humanity's spiritual evolution from ape to angel: "Arise and fly / The reeling Faun, the sensual feast; / Move upward, working out the beast, / And let the ape and tiger die."[23] Tennyson, a more consistent thinker than Lampman, accepted the implications of his views: human beings, as capable of shaping their own destiny, are obliged to escape nature if it is amoral. Occasionally, Lampman tried to resolve his ambivalence about the animal energies in human nature by accepting an inclusive view, and in "Man's Future" (1898), he prophesies an integration, rather than an exclusion, of qualities: "But man is still unfinished: many an age / Must bear him slowly onward stage by stage / In long adjustment,—mind and flesh and soul / Finally balanced to a rhythmic whole" (*ALS,* 34). In general, though, his progressive idealism sorts incongruously with his Romantic pastorals. Harry Levin has remarked, "If we reject the present, we must choose between the past and the future, between an Arcadian retrospect and a Utopian prospect."[24] Lampman's eagerness to go either way is a measure of the distress he felt in the conditions of his lifetime.

Lampman's intellectual position tended to be idealistic and austere, and his meliorist visions lack the sensuous intensity essential to his nature poems and love poems. The latter kinds, on the other hand, are quite similar in motive, form, and detail. Some of his more stylized landscapes (like many of Keats's early poems) eventually discover a nymph or maenad, usually in terms that are distinctly erotic. Conversely, his love poems often picture his beloved in terms of the freshness and beauty of nature. More than a century earlier, Edmund Burke, in his *Enquiry into the Sublime and Beautiful,* had linked his idea of beauty to attributes of the female form. Somewhat later, Shelley, in his prose fragment "On Love," suggested that a preoccupation with landscape may be an expression of displaced human love—a notion in interesting accord with Lampman's shift from one theme to the other in the eighties and again in the nineties.

Such an interpretation of Lampman's nature poetry is, of course, appropriate only up to a point. Landscape was for him, as for all Romantic poets, a way of exploring consciousness, and what he found was a wide and subtle range of meaning—aesthetic, moral, mythical, and religious. His spontaneous delight in natural beauty and sensuous experience expresses much more than a sublimation of sexual instinct. We see a larger and more resolved relation to nature, especially when he abandons pastoral and renders his native landscape specifically and accurately. He loved the distinctly unpastoral Canadian wilderness, which he explored on his canoe trips in the company of friends. Occasionally, the northern forest struck him as vaguely menacing, cold, and alien. In his sonnet "In the Wilds" (1897), however, the wilderness rouses his latent sense of identity with it:

> We run with rushing streams that toss and spume;
> We speed or dream upon the open meres;
> The pine-woods fold us in their pungent gloom;
> The thunder of wild water fills our ears;
> The rain we take, we take the beating sun;
> The stars are cold above our heads at night;
> On the rough earth we lie when day is done,
> And slumber even in the storm's despite.
> The savage vigour of the forest creeps
> Into our veins, and laughs upon our lips;
> The warm blood kindles from forgotten deeps,
> And surges tingling to the finger tips.
> The deep-pent life awakes and bursts its bands;
> We feel the strength and goodness of our hands.
>
> (*PAL,* 294–95)

Here erotic sublimation is in due proportion to other powerful feelings and a general sense of well-being. In "The Woodcutter's Hut" (1893), Lampman had expressed this physical apprehension of a fullness in life even more finely: "The animal man in his warmth and vigour, sound, and hard, and complete" (*PAL*, 249). Such passages counterpoint the spiritual and sexual distress more or less evident elsewhere in his work.

These contradictions reflect, among other things, Lampman's lack of concern over them. He was apparently of two minds about the proper relation of poetry to philosophy. On the one hand, he expresses his disinclination for intellectual rigor more than once, most obviously in his sonnet "The Truth" (1887). On the other hand, he insists in 1885 that "the great poet must be a broad and noble thinker."[25] And in 1891 he writes, "I have clothed myself in severity, and am working through Lewis' [*sic*] History of Philosophy. I was becoming weary of my ignorance about such things."[26] In a "Mermaid Inn" essay of 25 June 1892, he argues that the distinction of great poets is "largeness of vision" and "that rare combination of philosophy and the poetic impulse in the highest degree" (*MI*, 97). In another column just about eight months later, however, he develops this appealing little parable about snowshoeing:

The supreme charm of this delightful exercise lies in the fact that, as in the case of imagination as compared with logic, or the poet compared with the scientific philosopher, the snowshoer is freed from all rules of any absolute system of procedure. Whereas the ordinary wayfarer must follow slowly and ploddingly the worn paths and beaten highways, he sets all guidance at defiance, and marches at the bidding of any whim over fields, over marshes, down valleys, wherever he will. (*MI*, 18 February 1893, 262)

In general, Lampman's poetry was shaped more by mood than by system. And in this respect, as in so much else, he reflects his era. The nineteenth-century successors to the early Romantics depart from them on precisely this ground. Blake, Wordsworth, and Shelley conceived of vision as a unifying power surpassing the abstract systems of philosophy, and their works show a formidable synthesizing capacity. By contrast, the Victorians are poets of multiplicity whose attempts to develop coherent visions are either dubiously successful, like Tennyson's, or radically experimental, like Browning's. In America, Emerson and Whitman went so far as to declare their incongruities a poetic virtue. And as Lampman's period approached, the British writer Alfred Austin, whose criticism he admired, argued, "The poet has unlimited privilege of splendid self-contradiction. He presents the feeling of the moment; and his greatness consists, not in adhering to that feeling, but in his manner of presenting it."[27] Fundamentally, Lampman agreed. In his "At the Mermaid Inn" column of 29 October 1892, he printed "The Cup of Life" (1889), one of his most pessimistic sonnets, along with "Amor Vitae" (1891), a rapturous celebration of natural beauty and lofty dreams, and commented: "No man is more sincere than the poet; yet no man is more given to expressing under different circumstances the most opposite sentiments" (MI, 180).

At the same time, there were more personal reasons for the contradictions in Lampman's work. The biographical evidence is incomplete, but it is clear that, while he wanted very much to affirm the sweetness of life and the virtue of hope, his circumstances often made it difficult. Poor health, financial worries, the death of a son, and a painful extramarital attachment took their toll. The effect of his life on his work may remain, finally, an area of conjecture; but it does go some way toward explaining his work's peculiarities. "Passion," for instance, is generally a pejorative word for Lampman, a demon to be exorcised. This attitude vitiates his affinities with those Romantic poets who regarded desire as an essentially creative force. Lampman usually comes closer to expressing a Victorian idealism as the motive of his poetry, though at times he does sound rather like a genteel Blake: "There is always a much greater moral danger to be apprehended from a thwarted ambition, a native mental energy curbed and repressed, than from any amount of freedom given to any natural and legitimate desire for action" (MI, 15 April 1893, 294). The qualification, "legitimate," is significant, but, in any case, this is the rational argument of prose, and the poetry tells a different story, typified by his reference in "The Largest Life, III" (1897) to "the currents of blind passion that appall" (PAL, 301). Such lines are often coupled, as this one is, with a highly principled admonition to "divinest self-forgetfulness" (PAL, 300).

Lampman's misgivings about passion are amplified in his various observations about Stoicism. He wrote a sonnet, "Stoic and Hedonist" (1894), in praise of the position, but the following year he also wrote, "Stoicism is not happiness. It is simply armed peace, an attitude barren and comfortless."[28] In the sonnets written for

Katherine Waddell and published as "A Portrait in Six Sonnets" in *At the Long Sault,* the poet's lady is admired in one as "a tender stoic" (*ALS,* 44), but she is praised in another, written several months later, for the vitality that "keeps her too human for the stoic's part" (*ALS,* 43). That Stoicism was an issue for Lampman is a clue to both his personality and writing. Despite his advocacy of an ideal of self-cultivation, he harbored a persistent mistrust of the self and of experience. In 1894 he could write "The True Life," a sonnet animated with passionate revolt against "A makeshift truce, whereby the soul denies / The birthright of a being bright and new / Puts on a mask and crushes down the true, / And lolls behind a fence of courteous lies" (*ALS,* 35). Two years later, he echoed these lines in "Peace," a poem with repression palpable in its stilted rhythms and language:

> Him only shall peace find
> ....
> Whose soul hath set aside
> Desire and hope..........
> ....
> This is to live in truth,
> To plant against the passions' dark control
> The spirit's birth-right of immortal youth,
> The simple standard of the soul.
> (*PAL,* 310–11)

Of what does youth consist, one wonders, if not desire and hope? The contrast between these lyrics is one more piece of evidence about the crucial emotional upheaval in Lampman's life between 1894 and 1896.

The Rejected Quest

Unlike most Romantics, who proceed through a troubled quest toward spiritual reintegration and whose poems become voyages of self-discovery, Lampman typically envisages ways of eliminating the dimensions of time and self, and the necessity of a quest. Only in the two early fairy tales, "Hans Fingerhut's Frog Lesson" and "The Fairy Fountain," both written around 1884, and in "The Story of an Affinity," written ten years later, does he create quest-narratives of an essentially Romantic kind. More often, he pictures such symbolic journeys as largely painful or futile and recoils from them. In "The Monk" (1886), a baffled lover wanders from town to town distraught, ". . . following in unhappy quest / Uncertain clues that ended like the rest" (*PAL*, 76); in the end, he recovers thanks to his lady's courage. "The Frogs," tutelary spirits in one of Lampman's best-known poems (1887), are "breathers of wisdom won without a quest" (*PAL*, 7). "A Midnight Landscape" (c. 1890) suggests to him a terrible darkness "Where the lost heroes of old dreams oppressed / Might still be wandering on some dolorous quest" (*PAL*, 271). And the solace that he discovers "In the Pine Groves" (1892) is relief from the arduous challenge of "the weary road" (*PAL*, 267).

In Romantic poetry, the symbolic journey generally leads toward the liberation of redeeming powers within the depths of the self. As in Lampman's "Alcyone," the poet's exploratory impulse turns inward, seeking its satisfaction "in the clear abyss of mind" (*PAL*, 178). Such a pattern, according to Northrop Frye, reverses certain long-established archetypes:

For the quest of the soul, the attaining of man's ultimate identity, the traditional metaphors were upward ones, following the movement of the ascension of Christ, though they were there even before the Psalmist lifted up his eyes to the hills. In Romanticism the main direction of the quest of identity tends increasingly to be downward and inward, toward a hidden basis or ground of identity between man and nature.[29]

Notwithstanding his nature poetry, Lampman favors the older metaphors of ascent, and "the clearer self" ultimately comes to mean a vanished self. In "Freedom" (1887), for example, his revulsion from the viciousness of society leads him "Up to the hills, where our tired hearts rest, / Loosen, and halt, and regather their dreams" (*PAL*, 19). In "An Ode to the Hills" (1893), which takes its epigraph from Psalm 121, he yearns to "seek your upward way," to make his hermitage among the peaks and become "Wide-seeing, passionless, immutably glad, / And strong like you" (*PAL*, 224–25). And in a "Mermaid Inn" essay of 30 April 1892, he described his ideal home as built either upon a hill where "vision passes to the utmost visible limit and projects itself into the immensity beyond," or within a valley where "the upward sweep of the enclosing hills . . . leads the mind out of itself, and conducts it to regions of morning, freshness, and beauty" (*MI*, 63). Lampman's hunger for transcendence was so powerful that it seized on at least four different strategies. Occasionally, it compelled something akin to a conventional piety, but more often it focused on natural beauty, or utopian conjectures, or romantic love.

Lampman used the same term "dream" to describe all these ways of transcendence, and in this sense they are dreams that obviate rather than motivate a quest. Many critics have noticed this key word in his vocabulary, and Sandra Djwa, especially, has illuminated its complexity.[30] No one, however, has fully charted the treacherous ambiguities of the term, which even within particular poems may have contrary meanings. Too often, one suspects that Lampman's critical sense slumbered as he dreamed, that he used the word on reflex rather than on reflection. On the other hand, in many poems it has precise significance, and in some where it is used in contrary senses, the paradox is effective as part of the design.

The meaning of the term is apt to perplex unless we bear in mind a distinction between dream as a nocturnal phenomenon and the use of the word as a metaphor. The striking thing about passages in Lampman that deal with actual dreams is that virtually all of them denote psychological crisis rather than creative power. Almost without exception, such dreams are ugly nightmares, or erotic visions from which the dreamer awakes to a painfully frustrated reality, or aggrieved and uncertain visions of a dead child. The Freudian view that dreams express motivational tension is obviously relevant to such poems, but they remain a minor context of the word in Lampman's work.

In most of Lampman's poetry, "dream" occurs as a metaphor, but the issue is complicated further by his use of this singular word in two utterly contrary metaphorical senses. One of these resembles Shelley's characteristic account of human experience, with its "doubt, chance, and mutability," as "life's unquiet dream" ("Hymn to Intellectual Beauty," 36). Lampman himself wrote a commentary on the life-as-dream metaphor in "At the Mermaid Inn," where he decries the wasted lives of those who pursue the chimera of wealth, as opposed to the poet who "attaches himself to no dream," but rather "endeavours to see life simply as it is, and to estimate every-

thing at its true value in relation to the universal and the infinite"
(*MI*, 2 April 1892, 45).

Lampman's primary use of "dream," however, is as a metaphor
at odds with both his descriptions of actual dreams and the metaphor
of life-as-dream. In much of his work, the word signifies a state of
mind that is equivalent to its expression in poetry, or music, or
painting. "Art-as-dream" is a suitable phrase for this metaphor, by
which the dream becomes identified with the poem itself. In several
of his essays, Lampman adumbrated an aesthetic theory that clarifies
this idea. He claims that the poet's special gift is an ability to see
the "abstract beauty" in phenomena, and he describes poetry as an
approximate representation of essences, whether inward or external.[31] This theory is useful as a way of dealing with the nineteenth-
century schism between subjectivity and objectivity through sus-
taining the poet's mimetic relation to things while leaving scope
for his creative powers of interpretation. Different sorts of poems
result from different proportions of mimetic intent and imaginative
force brought to the subject, although those richer in the latter
quality are more apt to be called dreams. Lampman's landscape
poems are the context of this privileged sense of the word, ranging
as they do from objective studies, especially in the sonnets, to highly
symbolic transfigurations. Nature offered him an infinitely varied
subject that remained comparatively tractable. Again and again, a
scene or season, with its effect upon him, is dissolved and recom-
posed in his literary solution, held in the tenuous stasis so characteristic of his work.

It is no coincidence, then, that he was at his best in the sonnet
and short lyric, forms admirably suited to express a stasis, at his
next best in mood pieces and meditations of middle length, and at
his weakest in longer works which admit the problems of time and
process. That he understood this quite well is shown in his fine
sonnet "Ambition" (1896), significantly titled "For Me" in one of
his manuscripts:

> I see the world in pride and tumult pass
>   Too bright with flame, too dark with phantasy,
> Its forces meet and mingle mass in mass,
>   A tangle of Desire and Memory.
> I see the labours of untiring hands
>   Closing at last upon a shadowy prize,

And Glory bear abroad through many lands
   Great names—I watching with unenvious eyes
From other lips let stormy numbers flow:
   By others let great epics be compiled;
For me, the dreamer, 'tis enough to know
   The lyric stress, the fervour sweet and wild:
I sit me in the windy grass and grow
   As wise as age, as joyous as a child.

(PAL, 295)

An earlier version entitled "The Choice" (c. 1895) can illustrate Lampman's frequent inversion of the "dream" metaphor: "The world goes by me an unfathomed stream / Too bright with flame, too dark with mystery, / A shadowy glory and an ancient dream" (*ALS*, 17). The term is pejorative as applied to the world of action rather than to the contemplative poet. Lampman preferred those dreams that took the form of lyrical visions, splendidly wrought, but alien to the shadowy world of human struggle, of great epic, and of Romantic mythmaking.

But, of course, the "lyric stress" was not enough for him. From the early eighties, Lampman felt a need to develop his talent, if not in an epic enterprise, at least in poems that would treat the relations of things as well as their essences. In such a venture he was testing not only his own limitations but the poetic current of his era as he understood it. In one essay, he observed, "In poetry this is a lyrical and meditative age. The drama is almost impossible."[32] Seeking a vehicle for his larger conceptions, he tried, successively, romantic narrative ("Arnulph" and "White Margaret"), a Keatsian tale ("The Monk"), dramatic monologues ("An Athenian Reverie" and "Vivia Perpetua"), a biblical verse drama ("David and Abigail"), visionary narrative ("The Land of Pallas"), and a domestic idyll in the manner of Wordsworth and Tennyson ("The Story of an Affinity").

With the exception of "An Athenian Reverie" and "The Story of an Affinity," the results are not impressive. Generally, Lampman's strong lyric identification with his central characters makes them transparent expressions of his own impulses, and, in certain cases, the effects are quite as contradictory as any in his lyric poetry. "An Athenian Reverie" and "Vivia Perpetua," for example, are both monologues delivered by characters who register values that the poet quite obviously shares. The first, however, is a sensuous pagan reverie on the richness of life, while the second, a portrait of the early Christian martyrs, becomes a narrative homily on ". . . the fraud and littleness of life, / God's goodness and the solemn joy of death" (PAL, 239).

The narrative poems are generally conditioned by the formula of sentimental romance. The heroes and heroines tend to be vacuous stereotypes, and the pattern of lost love and found love to be artlessly spun out for the sake of the happy ending. One work, however, almost transcends these conventions through infusing the unlikely vehicle of the domestic idyll with the force of myth. "The Story of an Affinity," Lampman's longest and most ambitious poem, is far worthier of serious consideration than critics have allowed. It constitutes Lampman's attempt, at the height of his career in 1894, to integrate the disparate elements in his poetry. Significantly, he exploits the quest pattern, which he usually rejected, in affirming romantic love as a principle of individual and social renovation that transcends the natural and political orders. "The Story of an Affinity," though by no means flawless, does represent a provisional coherence in Lampman's vision. Regrettably, it did not lead to a greater poetic achievement. Personal disillusionment and declining health curbed Lampman's creative activity in the ensuing years, and "At the Long Sault" (1898–99), whatever its merits, is insufficient evidence of a new start just before the end.

Nevertheless, the rewards of reading him are considerable if we address the question of influence without prejudice, and if we put by expectations of a systematic vision. Lampman will remain of interest, not despite his contradictions, but because of them; because of the pathos in his life and early death; and because, finally, he made a substantial contribution to Canadian poetry. Some of his lyrics are Canadian classics, and many more are permanently enjoyable for their subtlety and beauty. Even his longer poems, especially "The Story of an Affinity," are worth attention as links between early nineteenth-century narrative verse in Canada and the more sophisticated work of E. J. Pratt and his successors in the twentieth century. Although Lampman's finely delineated dreams have their incongruities, like most dreams they can touch the imagination and revive the spirit. By this measure—his own—he succeeds.

Chapter Three
Nature Poetry

Poetic Interpretation

However else they differ, Lampman's critics have generally agreed upon the sensitivity and accuracy of his nature poems. Indeed, one of his earliest admirers, the prominent botanist and ornithologist John Macoun, praised *Among the Millet* for its naturalistic truth when it appeared in 1888.[1] But beyond its sharp perceptions and emphasis on local detail, Lampman's work reveals an essentially Romantic pattern of development. Like Wordsworth, Keats, and the English critic John Ruskin, he gradually moved from an almost obsessive interest in landscape to a greater concern with ethical and social questions. In 1891 he declared: "for the poet the beauty of external nature and the aspects of the most primitive life are always a sufficient inspiration."[2] This conviction inspired some of his best poems, but was corroded and qualified before his brief life ended eight years later.

Romantic nature poetry is not an easily defined genre, but a series of varied responses to a complex cultural crisis. Ruskin had observed the unprecedented importance of nature in nineteenth-century art and, in the third volume of *Modern Painters* (1856), had offered several explanations. In the first place, the development of natural science had stimulated greater interest in the environment. In the second, the ugliness of a newly urbanized society and the accelerated organization of human life in cities had fostered a hunger for whatever beauty and freedom remained in countryside or wilderness. Most fundamental of all, the waning of conventional religious belief had led many artists to seek a visionary meaning in the natural world. In Canada, Lampman's generation of poets was the first to express a genuinely Romantic sense of nature. In part this was because religious orthodoxy was more tenacious in the intellectual life of the colony than it was in the Old Country. As a professor at University College in Toronto ironically observed in 1887: "Men may venture on sayings in the orthodox precincts of Oxford that dare not be whispered in the State University of Ontario."[3] Also, it was only by Lampman's time that the land had been sufficiently tamed to allow a sympathetic view of it. In this regard the great symbolic event was the completion of the Canadian Pacific Railway, spanning the continent, in 1885.

Lampman's essay "Poetic Interpretation" provides a suggestive introduction to his practice. He considers anyone who responds to beauty a "poetic observer" (*SP,* 87), and he defines poets as those who possess this quality in a strength that compels expression. Although he is concerned with the aesthetic dimension of the world and life in general, his argument is developed largely in terms of landscape imagery. Significantly, he compares "the poetic soul" to "a vast musical instrument," an analogy also favored by the English Romantic poets. In their work this analogy is expressed in the symbol of the Aeolian harp, an instrument designed to produce musical sounds when set in an open breeze. Lampman probably remembered Shelley's use of the symbol in "A Defence of Poetry," where the wind represents experience and the harp the human mind, at once passively sensitive and actively responsive. Lampman similarly thinks of the poetic soul as a wind-harp that responds with varying degrees of fidelity to the particulars of experience, and he emphasizes the part played by "the interpreting poet." Of course, "interpretation" is the most ambiguous of terms, suggesting both the discovery of some outward truth and a unique "construction" by the interpreter. In Lampman's nature poetry this ambiguity is expressed in a shifting balance between the literal and the symbolic, and in a variable emphasis upon observed landscape and observing poet.

Another important statement occurs in Lampman's essay "The Character and Poetry of Keats," where Keats is praised for "that exquisite sense, which he above all others bred into English poetry, of the convertibility of all kinds of ideas into terms of the subtlest impressions gathered from field and forest and sky and sea."[4] Lampman's own method could be similarly described, for though his nature lyrics yield recurring patterns of meaning, they are more remarkable for their variety. That he saw various things in his precursors is made clear in the conclusion to this essay:

This "Ode to Autumn" has had a great part in creating that love for nature poetry, as we call it, that distinguishes the present generation. We have learned from Wordsworth a pure and solemn veneration for the grandeur and beauty of earth and sky; in Shelley this impulse glowed up into a sort of wild and transfiguring passion; but Keats is the representative of another phase which is perhaps nearer to the common heart than either, the genial love of the outward things of this earth—the mood of sensitive and luxurious delight.

Whatever merit this statement may have as a generalization about literary history, it accurately reflects Lampman's affinities: "To Autumn" is unquestionably the single poem that had the greatest part in creating his love of nature poetry, though Wordsworth's general influence upon him rivals Keats's. Ironically, "To Autumn" represents a very late stage in Keats's coming to terms with the world. In his "Epistle to John Hamilton Reynolds" (1818), the English poet had recorded an appalled vision of nature as "eternal fierce destruction," and in his early work the persistently stylized scenery and pastoral artifice suggest a deliberate evasion of the actual environment. Nevertheless, Lampman preferred Keats and Wordsworth over Shelley because both retained a faith (however qualified) in the intrinsic worth of natural things. As some critics have pointed out, Shelley's ostensible homage to nature does not stand up to scrutiny: he generally seeks to supplant the realm of nature by converting landscape into a densely symbolic structure. What is distinctive in his view of nature is the sense of a forbidding order alien to human perception and desire. Lampman eventually saw and condemned this attitude. In his student essay "The Revolt of Islam," he misread Shelley as "a pure worshipper of nature," but later he criticized him for failing to interpret nature accurately: "Into every picture that he drew, into every thought that he expressed, he wrought the strange unreal colour and the wild spiritual music, natural to his own beautiful but fantastic imagination. It is not actual nature that he interprets, but Shelley's powerful re-creation of it."[5]

In general, Lampman cultivated two kinds of nature poetry. In one, he creates vivid evocations of a place, or a time of year or of day. The features of the scene, charged with sensuous detail, dominate the poem, and the poet keeps a low profile: his characteristic attitude is empathy, and his mood is identified with the complexion of the landscape. In the other, the poet appears in high profile in the landscape, and experiences a sense of separation from as well as relation to the scene; his characteristic attitude is meditative, and the meanings of the landscape are made more explicit. A distinctive sense of time accompanies each of these modes. In the first, time is congruent with natural process or emotional rhythm. In the second, the speaker's conventional sense of time as linear and abstract is transfigured in an epiphany, the unforeseen moment when the imagination penetrates the appearances of nature.

These different modes correspond to Geoffrey Hartman's distinction between the kind of landscape created by Keats in "To Autumn" and the treatment of landscape more characteristic of Wordsworth. Hartman's term for poetry of the first sort is "Hesperian" art, from the classical name for the evening star that appears in the west. He proposes that such poetry is a more genuine expression of Western sensibility than epiphanic poetry, which has its roots in Oriental religious thought, and he claims that Hesperian poetry arrived in England with William Collins's "Ode to Evening" (1746). While resisting the temptation to apply this hypothesis fully to such a westerly poet as Lampman, I think that Hartman's distinction can illuminate the different moods and structures in Lampman's nature lyrics. According to Hartman, the effect of a Hesperian sensibility is:

to ripen the pictorial quality of the poem rather than to evoke astonishment. The emphasis is on self-forgetful relaxation . . . not on saturnine fixation. No more than in "To Evening" is nature epiphanic: Keats's autumn is not a specter but a spirit, one who steals over the landscape, or "amid her store" swellingly imbues it. The poet's mind is not rapt or astonished and so forced back on itself by a sublime apparition.[6]

As Hartman's language implies, and as some of his other essays confirm, this analysis is essentially a revaluation of the eighteenth-century categories of the Beautiful and the Sublime. The Sublime has always had religious connotations, and in its original meaning an epiphany is the manifestation of divinity. The epiphany in Romantic poetry signifies the imagination's revelation of itself as supreme, through the transformation of the natural realm in which it works. In a Hesperian mood, on the other hand, though the poet may discover gods, they will be partial and local aspects of nature: the tutelary spirits of the place, the season, or the time of day.

Hesperian Moods

Lampman's works in the Hesperian style range from descriptive studies of the Ontario countryside, through impressionistic views, to mythopoeic landscapes. Most of his primarily descriptive poems are sonnets—a form that he found ideal for clarifying his aesthetic sense of nature. Indeed, they are "sonnet-landscapes," as he termed the work of a contemporary in a review that supplies a judgment proper to his own poems: "They are true pictures, clear and fresh from nature, with the very earth savour in them."[7] Some, like "April Night" (c. 1888), evoke a sense of stasis and satisfaction through a repletion of detail. Others, like "A Dawn on the Lièvre" (c. 1889) and "A January Morning" (1889?), describe some change in the scene, proceeding structurally through a transfiguration. The titles of many such sonnets indicate their essentially mimetic character. "Among the Orchards" (1889) is a virtuoso study in contrasts, while "A Thunderstorm" (1890) vividly re-creates the impression of that familiar occurrence: the moment of anticipation shattered by a peal of thunder, and followed by the steadying rhythm of the downpour.

Generally, these sonnets are charged with a sensuous richness in which sight and sound are amplified by texture and atmosphere. Lampman seems to have had an extraordinary eye for the protean phenomena of nature. His journals describing excursions into the wilderness show the same sensitivity to minute particulars that animates his poetry, and that contributed to his interest in painting.[8] His "Mermaid Inn" column of 16 April 1892, coauthored with Duncan Campbell Scott, is a detailed review of that year's Royal Canadian Academy exhibition. Significantly, Lampman and Scott note the general superiority of the landscape paintings included in the exhibition, and praise the "absolute verisimilitude" and "truth of observation" achieved in the best pictures (*MI,* 55).

The range of Lampman's visual response to scenery can be sketched in relation to two centuries of landscape art. "Evening" (c. 1889), for example, is largely eighteenth-century in its literary and pictorial qualities. In language and detail it goes back beyond the Romantics to Thomas Gray and William Collins. Indeed, it treats the same subject as the latter's famous "Ode," which Hartman identified as the progenitor of Hesperian art in England. In the way it works up its subject, this sonnet may strike us as being among the least original of Lampman's landscapes:

From upland slopes I see the cows file by,
Lowing, great-chested, down the homeward trail,
By dusking fields and meadows shining pale
With moon-tipped dandelions. Flickering high,
A peevish night-hawk in the western sky
Beats up into the lucent solitudes,
Or drops with griding wing. The stilly woods
Grow dark and deep and gloom mysteriously.
Cool night winds creep, and whisper in mine ear.
The homely cricket gossips at my feet.
From far-off pools and wastes of reeds I hear,
Clear and soft-piped, the chanting frogs break sweet
In full Pandean chorus. One by one
Shine out the stars, and the great night comes on.
                                        (*PAL*, 198–99)

The tinge of melancholy, the classical allusion, and the domesticity
are all conventions of the age of sensibility that preceded Romanticism. "Evening" is the literary equivalent of a Gainsborough painting—"Landscape with Bridge," for example, which also confronts
us with perambulatory cows. The conventional imagery and diction
are qualities with which our own age has perhaps permanently lost
sympathy. But "Evening" nevertheless has formal merits which
characterize many of Lampman's very different sonnets. The poet's
eye moves from the foreground through the middle distance to the
background of sky and soaring hawk; then the hawk's swoop parallels
the movement of his attention back from sky to earth. The subsequent details repeat the alternation of near and far, expanding
toward the final cosmic framing of the scene; and the image of stars
against the night echoes the "moon-tipped dandelions" in the dusky
fields of the poem's opening. The sonnet organizes the observer's
sense of distance in a graceful movement like the focal line of a
landscape painting, or a musical phrase. In fact there is a melodic
as well as a visual pattern in "Evening."

"A Niagara Landscape," composed the same year, is more akin
to the landscape painting of Lampman's own time:

Heavy with haze that merges and melts free
    Into the measureless depth on either hand,
    The full day rests upon the luminous land
In one long noon of golden reverie.

Now hath the harvest come and gone with glee.
    The shaven fields stretch smooth and clean away,
    Purple and green, and yellow, and soft gray,
Chequered with orchards. Farther still I see
Towns and dim villages, whose roof-tops fill
    The distant mist, yet scarcely catch the view.
Thorold set sultry on its plateau'd hill,
        And far to westward, where yon pointed towers
    Rise faint and ruddy from the vaporous blue,
        Saint Catharines, city of the host of flowers.
                                        (*PAL*, 272–73)

The eighteenth century persists in the faint personification of "day" and there is an echo of Shelley in the sixth line, but in its emphasis on the transitory appearance of the countryside under the play of light and atmosphere, this poem suggests the art of Monet or Renoir. The impression of distance and of an expansive, upward movement leads the sensory eye toward visionary insight, and indeed this noontide reverie yields its epiphany in the sacramental pun of its final line. Such meanings often enrich Lampman's sonnets, but they are made secondary to his artistry. His "sonnet-landscapes" require that we temper our demand for ideas with an appreciation of form, and that we sustain an awareness of the richly sensuous texture even as we are tempted to anatomize the technique.

A third sonnet differs again from both "Evening" and "A Niagara Landscape," as a startling anticipation of a phase of landscape painting that developed some twenty years after Lampman's death. "On Lake Temiscamingue" was inspired during his camping trip to northern Ontario in 1896, and it shares with some other late works a keen perception of that region which is largely absent from Lampman's earlier nature poetry. The octave arranges a picture through the painter's eye for color and composition; the sestet enlarges our imaginative response in its appeal to our sense of sound and motion:

A single dreamy elm, that stands between
    The sombre forest and the wan-lit lake,
Halves with its slim gray stem and pendent green
    The shadowed point. Beyond it without break
Bold brows of pine-topped granite bend away,
    Far to the southward, fading off in grand
Soft folds of looming purple. Cool and gray,

> The point runs out, a blade of thinnest sand.
> Two rivers meet beyond it: wild and clear,
>   Their deepening thunder breaks upon the ear—
> The one descending from its forest home
>   By many an eddied pool and murmuring fall—
> The other cloven through the mountain wall,
>   A race of tumbled rocks, a roar of foam.
>
>   (*PAL,* 293)

Rather than manipulating imported conventions or seeking to transcend the data of sense perception, Lampman here attempts to identify the actual qualities of the Canadian wilderness. The sense of loneliness and of conflict among powerful elements prefigures the Canadian landscape poems of F. R. Scott and A. J. M. Smith, as well as the paintings of the Group of Seven; the "single dreamy elm" anticipates the foregrounded tree that is virtually their signature. Considered as a series, "Evening," "A Niagara Landscape," and "On Lake Temiscamingue" reflect the gradual naturalization of Lampman's landscape art, in two senses of the word: on the one hand, a subordination of poetic convention to mimetic precision; on the other, a greater emphasis upon the distinctive features of the Canadian locale.

The pictorial method in nature poetry is well suited to sonnets and brief lyrics. In longer pieces it may lapse into what Coleridge termed "*anatomy* of description (a fault not uncommon in descriptive poetry)."[9] The most successful of Lampman's longer nature poems amplify the rendered scene through symbolic design or through a meditation by which the perceived landscape becomes conceptually meaningful. Those in blank verse and ballad form often introduce Wordsworthian concerns with memory or morality. Those written in more intricate stanza forms—reminiscent of Keats's experiments in the great odes—sustain a more Hesperian atmosphere, but also discover some significance in nature re-presented.

In Lampman's more elaborate mythopoeic landscapes, the natural cycle of the seasons provides the central imagery and structure. In such poems as "April," "June," "September," and "Winter," he continues a tradition that descends from classical literature, permeates Middle English and Renaissance art, and approaches his time through the poetry of James Thomson, Blake, Shelley, and Keats. His relation to this tradition is the central theme of "June" (1890).

The first five stanzas of this poem accumulate a veritable naturalist's inventory of flowers and woodland creatures, though with increasing emphasis on the "magic" of these things when they are intensely felt absences or presences. Then a fleeting vision of the month "in living form of flesh" ushers in an erotic myth:

> Before me like a mist that streamed and fell
>   All names and shapes of antique beauty passed
> In garlanded procession with the swell
>   Of flutes between the beechen stems; and last,
>
> I saw the Arcadian valley, the loved wood,
>   Alpheus stream divine, the sighing shore,
>   And through the cool green glades, awake once more,
> Psyche, the white-limbed goddess, still pursued,
>   Fleet-footed as of yore,
> The noonday ringing with her frighted peals,
>   Down the bright sward and through the reeds she ran,
> Urged by the mountain echoes, at her heels
>   The hot-blown cheeks and trampling feet of Pan.
>   (*PAL*, 142–43)

The seasonal phenomena so lovingly observed earlier in the poem are mutable, and they veil their meanings; in the end the poet shapes them to a vision charged with archetypal meaning. But for the poet of Lampman's time, such dreams must be ambiguous and tenuous. The elusive figures in his landscapes embody an intuition of unity in the teeming diversity of nature; and they illustrate the power of the human spirit to unify its ostensible chaos of emotion, sensation, and perception. They are figures in poetry, the dimension where nature and spirit meet: the figures of personification, metaphor, symbol, and myth.

This borderland is the special province of Hesperian art, which suggests immanence rather than transcendence, and which makes mortality a part of its scheme. Lampman therefore embraces the meanings of autumn and winter as well as those of spring and summer. His seasons poems extend to all four phases the theme of Keats's "To Autumn": "Where are the songs of Spring? Aye, where are they? / Think not of them, thou hast thy music too—." The imagery of sexual energy that assumes a mythological form at the end of "June" suffuses Lampman's Spring and Summer poems, suggesting potency in the former, and fullness in the latter. The Autumn poems are elegiac, emphasizing loss and mortality, and the Winter poems embody a principle of necessity or fatality that is the only equal of sexual power in the universe. Generally, Lampman sees the seasons as complementary, fulfilling and completing each other, and throughout his nature poetry the presiding qualities of one season are apt to appear as secondary qualities in another. In "April" (1884), autumn appears as a maidservant to Eros, preparing a bed for the sexual arousal of spring:

> The old year's cloaking of brown leaves, that bind
> The forest floor-ways, plated close and true—
> The last love's labour of the autumn wind—
> Is broken with curled flower buds white and blue
> In all the matted hollows, and speared through
> With thousand serpent-spotted blades up-sprung,
> Yet bloomless, of the slender adder-tongue.
>
> (PAL, 5)

Conversely, mortality is present at the high tide of life. "June" begins with an enumeration of the spring-flowers that have already passed: "gone are the wind-flower and the adder-tongue" (PAL, 140). The same duality appears in "Winter" (1885), a marvelously inventive poem. The season is imagined in traditional terms as a capricious conqueror who terrorizes the land; but the terror is much mitigated by the humor of Lampman's details:

> The Winter speeds his fairies forth and mocks
>   Poor bitten men with laughter icy cold,
>   Turning the brown of youth to white and old
>   With hoary-woven locks,
> And gray men young with roses in their cheeks.
>
> (PAL, 25)

Winter is not only a despot but also an artist and a dreamer: he is a parodist, a mocker of mortal presumption. The season actually brings vigorous correction to the overripe languor of summer: "The long days came and went; the riotous bees / Tore the warm grapes in many a dusty vine, / And men grew faint and thin with too much ease, / And Winter gave no sign" (PAL, 24). "September" (1890) likewise sees a liberation in the passing of summer from "the tilled earth, with all its fields set free" (*PAL*, 154). In this respect, Lampman's seasons poems recall William Blake's vision of the principles of existence in "The Marriage of Heaven and Hell":

Thus one portion of being, is the Prolific, the other, the Devouring: to the devourer it seems as if the producer was in his chains, but it is not so, he only takes portions of existence and fancies that the whole.

But the Prolific would cease to be Prolific unless the Devourer as a sea received the excess of his delights. (plate 16)

The Hesperian quality of Lampman's seasons poems is reflected in the sense of time conveyed through his marvelous variations of rhythm and stanza. The protracted scope of the seasons effectively precludes the sudden disjunction of epiphany. In Spring poems such as "April" and "The Frogs," time slows and eddies as the stanzas gather sensuous detail and the poet savours the music and visual richness of the landscape. In "June," time slows through a similar accumulation of fragrance, color, and sound, then advances more briskly, then races with the pursuit of Psyche by Pan. In "September" time ebbs to an interval of "perfect clarity," an extended pause typical of the Autumn poems. In "Winter," time moves capriciously to the tune of the tyrant's whim. Almost always, such poems suggest the rhythms of natural process or of emotional response, a consequence of the poet's immersion in the scene.

The central meaning of Lampman's seasons myth turns on the word "dream," and is complete in as early a poem as "Ballade of Summer's Sleep," composed in 1883 and published in *Among the Millet*. (Lampman's earliest extant poem, an unpublished lyric titled "The Stream," dated 1878 in manuscript, deals with the same theme.) Though not the best of its kind, "Ballade of Summer's Sleep" clarifies both the fundamental meaning of the myth and its essential limitations. The central role is taken by the Dreams that attend Summer's sleep as the repository of creative power during the barren winter. The poet shares this redeeming power and expresses it in his art, "under the influence of the same eternal spirit that moulded and constructed the universe," as Lampman wrote in "At the Mermaid Inn" (*MI*, 126). A large number of Lampman's poems rehearse this myth of potency. It is the ultimate meaning that he found in nature, and not a trivial one. But despite its universality and power to move us, the drama of seasonal death and regeneration is a limited drama, a rudimentary mythology liable to collapse into clichéd personification and metaphorical embellishment unless it is related more closely to human experience. This danger is registered in the very form of the "Ballade," with its technical brilliance producing a closed circle of repetition and minor variation.

Collectively, Lampman's seasons poems illustrate this circumscription, though it is to his credit that he succeeds so often in such a fundamentally limited genre. When he comes to relate his seasons myth more closely to human life, he confronts the problem of human consciousness. The aesthetic dimension of his nature poems acquires a greater psychological depth, and his sense of oneness with nature is unsettled, when the emphasis shifts from the external landscape to the poet's point of view.

Epiphanic Meanings

"Winter Hues Recalled" (c. 1888) is a paradigm of epiphanic landscape poetry. Although the language is occasionally Keatsian, the manner and theme of this long meditation in blank verse are unmistakeably Wordsworthian. It begins with some two dozen discursive lines on the value of spontaneous recollection, the "treasure of hours gone" that lies hidden "in the quiet garner-house of memory," only to emerge when the will relaxes and the mind idles (*PAL*, 27). The poem's sacramental language suggests its concern with the Romantic epiphany, the post-Christian moment of communion wherein nature yields a sublime vision. The prologue is followed by the speaker's description of his recent involuntary memory of just such an experience; then the poem proceeds through its longest section to describe the earlier occasion of this "moment." Here, then, is a complex, even contorted structuring of time very unlike that in the seasons poems. We are made aware of (1) the meditative present, which incorporates (2) the recent past, in which the flash of memory occurred, and (3) the epiphany in the distant past, remembered not only lately (2), but also now (1). The original occasion, an excursion in the winter countryside, passed through three phases: the speaker's "unobservant" ramble toward "the loftiest level of the snow-piled fields," the epiphany he experienced at this height of land, and his return to a normal state of mind as the moment passed. Time in this poem emerges as an abstraction of diverse modes of awareness rather than as a mood conditioned by sensuous natural rhythms.

This abstraction of time is accompanied by the transfiguration of space in the poet's epiphany, the spot of time preserved in his subconscious. On his outward journey through the snowscape, the seasonal forces and colors had appeared in a shifting balance reminiscent of the Hesperian lyrics, but when he reached the hilltop and paused to rest, he was struck by a change of color which had gradually harmonized fields, hills, forests, and all the details of the scene:

> The whole broad west was like a molten sea
> Of crimson. In the north the light-lined hills
> Were veiled far off as with a mist of rose
> Wondrous and soft. Along the darkening east
> The gold of all the forests slowly changed
> To purple. In the valley far before me,
> Low sunk in sapphire shadows, from its hills,
> Softer and lovelier than an opening flower,
> Uprose a city with its sun-touched towers,
> A bunch of amethysts.
>
> (PAL, 29–30)

Such distanced visions of a city recur in Lampman's poetry; what is striking here is the movement up and out of rather than outward and into the particulars of nature. The epiphany ends as the sun sets:

> Like one spell-bound
> Caught in the presence of some god, I stood . . .
> [and] saw the arc of rose
> Rise ever higher in the violet east,
> Above the frore front of the uprearing night
> Remorsefully soft and sweet. Then I awoke
> As from a dream, and from my shoulders shook
> The warning chill, till then unfelt, unfeared.
>
> (PAL, 30)

We may recall Hartman's comment that "the East . . . is epiphanic country" where "the poet's mind is . . . forced back on itself by a sublime apparition."[10] Lampman's risen god remains unspecified, in lower-case, and confined to a simile, but nevertheless transcends both reason and landscape. In one sense, this god is the imagination itself, which embraces and resolves all contradictions. The paradoxes multiply, however, when we consider that after all the sun does set, the god vanishes, the chill returns. If "Winter Hues Recalled" dramatizes Lampman's aesthetic faith, it also acknowledges the inevitable return to mutable life from the timeless moment of art; yet even this descent is made part of the poem. Sunset is a persistent image in Lampman's work, often pictured against a line of trees or towers, and associated with a dying king or god. In counterpoint to the omnipotent sun and enduring noon of such poems as "The Frogs" and "Heat," sunset becomes an emblem of mortality, frustration, and the limits of imagination. In its epiphanic meaning, it is contrary to the quintessential Hesperian image of evening, which connotes reconciliation, continuity, peace, and hope.

The affirmation of a religious significance in nature persists throughout *The Poems of Archibald Lampman.* In the sonnet "A Prayer" (1887), the poet turns for strength and light not to the Deity but to a source immemorially given feminine gender in myth and poetry: "O Earth, O dewy mother, breathe on us / Something of all thy beauty and thy might" (*PAL,* 109). In this reverence for the maternal principle Lampman is at one with Wordsworth, and would incur the wrath that the latter's "natural piety" provoked in William Blake: "I see in Wordsworth the Natural Man rising up against the Spiritual Man Continually, and then he is No Poet but a Heathen Philosopher."[11] Perhaps it is worth noting that Blake himself has incurred censure for the antifeminist implications of his prophecies, a risk run by any writer whose myth-making envisages male and female principles. In any case, "A Prayer" reflects Lampman's desire to sustain the general revision of Christian attitudes entered upon by the English Romantics.

This undertaking is especially evident in *Lyrics of Earth,* and in one of that volume's poems it issues in a particularly daring image. "The Moon-Path" (1889) tells how the beauty of moonlight on the sea awakened the poet to the marvelous appeal of the pagan myths and a vision of the gods and "goddesses of old," and its final lines imply that through such an access of imagination, the poet becomes his own Redeemer (*PAL,* 147). "Life and Nature," another "lyric of earth" composed in the same month, interprets Christianity as essentially a psychological reaction to human suffering. The Sunday worship of an institutional faith fails to satisfy the speaker, who turns to nature for a sustenance that he cannot find in organized forms of religion. He rediscovers joy in a meadow where green earth and blue sky issue in life itself, and where the birds offer a joyous music that contrasts with the shrill moanings of the church organ in the city. This is not escapism, as some of Lampman's critics might suggest. Several of his nature poems do invite the charge, but by far the greater number merit the distinction that Wordsworth made in "Tintern Abbey" when he recalled that on his first journey to the Wye he was "more like a man / Flying from something that he dreads than one / Who sought the thing he loved." Revisiting the banks of the Wye, Wordsworth sought what he loved, the "tranquil restoration" of natural beauty; and like Lampman, he also came from "the din / Of towns and cities."

The spiritual regeneration that the poet finds in the natural world after a depressing interval "in city pent," becomes a distinctive topos in Romantic literature, though it emerges from the much older tradition of pastoral poetry. The significance of the city in Lampman's poetry deserves separate comment, but one or two points can be made here. The city is the center not only of institutional religion but also of secular authority and commerce. One of the primary functions of pastoral poetry is criticism of these secular institutions, and this function persists when stylized pastoral scenery gives way to Romantic natural landscape. The Romantic poet discovers his identity with the quickening forces of nature rather than in social hierarchy and law, and thereby is freed to assume a critical perspective on tyranny and corruption in the society around him. Nature poetry for Lampman, as for Wordsworth, had not only aesthetic and religious significance, but also moral implications. His late sonnet, "To the Ottawa River" (1898) is an explicitly moral reading of landscape: the river becomes a symbol of the strength by which both nature and the human spirit survive enslavement and profiteering in a materialistic age. Similarly, in "Man and Nature" (c. 1890) Lampman suggests that natural beauty is doubly precious because it is one of the few things that remain abundant and free in an era of commercial exploitation.

For Lampman, then, nature not only yields a sublime vision that comforts and exalts the spirit, but also directly influences the moral lives of men and women. His most explicit affirmation of this belief occurs in the sonnet "On the Companionship with Nature" (1892),

designed as a response to Wordsworth's indictment of men for their
disregard of nature in "The World is Too Much with Us" (1807).
Through his form, idiom, and tone, and in a specific echo in the
ninth line, Lampman evokes Wordsworth's sonnet and thereby implies an understanding of his own role as an heir to the English
Romantic.

> Let us be much with Nature; not as they
> That labour without seeing, that employ
> Her unloved forces, blindly without joy;
> Nor those whose hands and crude delights obey
> The old brute passion to hunt down and slay;
> But rather as children of one common birth,
> Discerning in each natural fruit of earth
> Kinship and bond with this diviner clay.
> Let us be with her wholly at all hours,
> With the fond lover's zest, who is content
> If his ear hears, and if his eye but sees;
> So shall we grow like her in mould and bent,
> Our bodies stately as her blessèd trees,
> Our thoughts as sweet and sumptuous as her flowers.
>
> (PAL, 258–59)

The eleventh line alludes to one of Lampman's favorite passages of
scripture, Matthew 13:16: "But blessed *are* your eyes, for they see:
and your ears, for they hear." Christ's parable refers to the kingdom
of heaven and the word of God, but Lampman means the beauty
of earth and the music of nature. The final lines recall Wordsworth's
"Fair seed-time had my soul" (1850 *Prelude*, I.301), among other
examples of this Romantic motif. The sonnet also recalls Wordsworth's famous quatrain in "The Tables Turned": "One impulse
from a vernal wood / May teach you more of man, / Of moral evil
and of good, / Than all the sages can." To surmise a full circle in
this pattern of relationships, I note that in "The Tables Turned"
Wordsworth's dictum is addressed, coincidentally or not, to a
schoolmaster friend named Matthew. Lampman's sense of a moral
influence in nature differs from Wordsworth's, however, in one
significant way: by and large it lacks the dimension of human
companionship found everywhere in Wordsworth's poetry. In "Tintern Abbey" Wordsworth crowns his meditation on a communion
with nature with an affirmation of the value of human communion,

as he offers a benediction to his sister Dorothy. Similarly, in the "Immortality Ode" and in "Resolution and Independence," he considers his relation to nature in the light of his relation to other people, and he devotes the eighth book of *The Prelude* to "Love of Nature Leading to Love of Man." Lampman is the more solitary, by far, in his major meditative landscape poems.

Chapter Four
Six Landscapes

Noontide

Pictorial moods and visionary meanings are often mixed in Lampman's poetry or shade into one another in varying degrees. In several of his finest poems the two merge in (what is almost a contradiction in terms) a lengthy epiphany. "The Frogs" (1887), "Heat" (1887), and "Among the Timothy" (1885) represent this extraordinary equilibrium in the image of a prolonged high noon, a landscape of spiritual peace under a stationary or barely moving sun.[1] These three poems stand out in the cycle of nature lyrics that occupies the opening pages of *Among the Millet*. They have attracted more comment than any other poems by Lampman, and they are the "dreams" par excellence of his nature poetry. However, the vision that they articulate was both too tenuous and too solitary to remain the basis of his work. Whatever the substance of an epiphany, its very form implies a necessary return to the more problematic norms of human perception and human life.

The idea of a protracted noon has numerous antecedents. Lampman's special use of the image is, in part, a drastic transformation of the motionless sun that, in the Old Testament, facilitates a righteous slaughter of the heathen (Joshua 10:12–14). A character in Lampman's dramatic poem "David and Abigail" makes this reference explicit in expressing the same attitude that pervades the nature lyrics in *Among the Millet*: "I would I had the power of Joshua, / Who stayed the hour and made the sun stand still, / So would I lie here in the pleasant grass, / And hold this morning freshness for an age . . ." (*PAL*, 398). In a study of the theme of midday in Italian literature, Nicholas J. Perella has stressed the ambiguous nature of the hour, which has long been associated not only with the fullness and triumph of imaginative strength, but also with the parching tyranny of a harsh outward reality.[2] In Christian tradition, "the destruction that wasteth at noonday" (Psalm 91:6) was linked to acedia, the spiritual desiccation that threatens the soul with despair and annihilation.[3] This baleful aspect of noontide appears in several of Lampman's poems, including "Among the Timothy," but generally gives way to illumination or rapture. Such moments of illumination also have a counterpart in Eastern philosophy, as expounded in some memorable remarks by Thoreau: "All laborers must have their nooning, and at this season of the day, we are all, more or less, Asiatics, and give over all work and reform. . . . There is a struggle between the oriental and the occidental in every nation; some who would be forever contemplating the sun, and some who are hastening toward the sunset."[4] Beyond their connections with these traditions, Lampman's three great poems of noontide are also strongly imbued with the spirit of the two romantic poets he loved best.

"The Frogs" (1887) marks the consummation of Keats's influence on Lampman. Such earlier poems as "The Hepatica" (1883) and "April" (1884) are interesting as exercises in the English poet's manner, but they offer little freshness or depth of vision. In "The Frogs" Lampman makes Keats not so much his model as his resource. While this poem strongly evokes the English poet's work, its echoes are more than a mere reflection of Lampman's taste: they form a meaningful pattern of allusion. In a sense, Lampman's poem is both the greeting of a kindred spirit and a direct response to Keats's odes, especially the "Ode on a Grecian Urn" and its famous final lines: " 'Beauty is truth, truth beauty,'—that is all / Ye know on earth, and all ye need to know." From the apostrophes with which both poems open, through their motifs and tonal modulations, to the enigmatic messages with which they close, "Ode on a Grecian Urn" and "The Frogs" represent an imaginative communion spanning an ocean and three quarters of a century. Their differences are equally important, though to what extent these differences indicate rivalry or "creative misreading" on Lampman's part is a difficult question.[5]

Fortunately, Lampman's essay on Keats, completed in 1893, states his understanding of "Ode on a Grecian Urn": "It is [Keats's] clearest expression of pure and happy trust in Beauty—Beauty as comprehending all things that the soul need care for. The effect upon the soul of a thing of perfect beauty is not so much that of completeness as of boundlessness like eternity. Thought cannot go beyond it, and must rest in its presence contented and absorbed. What can it be therefore but Truth, or, as Keats thought, the only absolute Truth?"[6]

Today many readers would probably agree that Lampman overlooks Keats's melancholy sense of the tension between art and life. His own poem articulates not so much a tension as a contrast between the states of "dream" and "discord." He also diverges from the form that Keats developed for his odes, and registers his imaginative independence in what is perhaps the most striking way he could: not through a further refinement of the sonnet structure, but through reverting to the sonnet itself and demonstrating his peculiar genius for making it, as a stanza, the fit vehicle for an extended meditation.

The opening sonnet-stanza of "The Frogs" evokes the shade of Keats's urn even as it introduces a different visionary theme. Lampman associates "dream" with a purposive principle in nature that cannot be known rationally, but that touches the human heart. When recognized and shared, this dream can free us from anguish through its revelation of an ultimate unity in the order and process of nature. The frogs in chorus are envisaged as "voices of earth" (to cite another of Lampman's titles). They communicate as music does, transcending the conceptual duplicities of human language:

> Breathers of wisdom won without a quest,
>> Quaint uncouth dreamers, voices high and strange,
>> Flutists of lands where beauty hath no change,
> And wintry grief is a forgotten guest,
> Sweet murmurers of everlasting rest,
>> For whom glad days have ever yet to run,
>> And moments are as aeons, and the sun
> But ever sunken half-way toward the west.
>
> Often to me who heard you in your day,
>> With close rapt ears, it could not choose but seem
> That earth, our mother, searching in what way
>> Men's hearts might know her spirit's inmost dream;
>>> Ever at rest beneath life's change and stir,
>>> Made you her soul, and bade you pipe for her.
>>>> (PAL, 7)

The epithets in the octave idealize the frogs as harbingers of paradise—that is, nature in its beauty and sufficiency, transfigured through the observer's purification. Like the ideal realm evoked by Keats's Grecian urn, this paradise is timeless; unlike that disembodied and constrained dimension, it is also sensual and fertile. The

"Ode on a Grecian Urn" expresses Keats's ambivalence toward art as well as toward life, and its undertone of sadness reflects the conviction that either world is enjoyed only at a price. In the first sonnet of "The Frogs," the speaker's reference to "wintry grief" hints at a similar subversion of his dream, and his use of the past tense, as well as the stressed and pivotal word *seem,* suggests that he may be dealing in illusions, and fated to suffer an estrangement from this paradise. Such references to the fallen world of normal experience persist through succeeding stanzas in counterpoint to the elaboration of his vision; indeed, the entire affirmation of "The Frogs" is poised against its potential negation. Consequently, we may be misled into anticipating the dissolution of that vision, especially if we think not only of the "Ode on a Grecian Urn," but also of Keats's "Ode to a Nightingale," as several passages invite us to do.

In the second, third, and fourth sonnets, the counterpoint between the dream of paradise and the world of discord is extended through two unequal movements, the stronger of which eventually absorbs the weaker. The world of mortality and loss is indicated by the death of the first spring flowers and through references to the passing days and seasons. In "The Frogs," however, these temporal cycles are curiously subverted: they are broken up, left incomplete, or merged. The suspended afternoon of I precedes the prolonged noontide of III, and the ripening springtime of II never really yields to summer or autumn. The "hours" of II and IV retain something of their classical identification with the seasons, and acquire a spatial character. Temporal images become less significant as measurements of time than as parts of a design. In the third sonnet, which marvelously renders the visionary stasis of noon, the frogs are described as omnipresent and motionless, "with eyes that dreamed beyond the night and day" (*PAL,* 8). Their voices accompany the poem's more powerful, prevailing movement, which is neither linear nor cyclic, but expansive: the extension, enrichment, and fulfillment of a mood. The most obvious feature of this pattern is the widening focus of the speaker's attention, from the buds and flowers in II, through a larger view of the terrestrial landscape in III, to the celestial firmament in IV. Lampman's technique complements this movement, through the leisurely, eddying effect of his tone and rhythm. The complex, graceful periods flow limpidly through the

formal conventions of the sequence, generating one sensuous, rounded
picture after another.

The structure of Lampman's poem differs fundamentally from the
structure of both the "Ode on a Grecian Urn" and the "Ode to a
Nightingale." Keats's poems have been well described as showing
a "steady advance and withdrawal," toward and away from vision.[7]
"The Frogs" confounds any expectation of such an outcome. We
may be led to anticipate the eventual dissolution of the dream, but
instead are left with its reaffirmation. The fifth and final sonnet
achieves this end through a transvaluation of terms:

> Morning and noon and midnight exquisitely,
>   Rapt with your voices, this alone we knew,
> Cities might change and fall, and men might die,
>   Secure were we, content to dream with you
>   That change and pain are shadows faint and fleet,
>   And dreams are real, and life is only sweet.
>   (*PAL*, 9–10)

These final lines probably are as endlessly debatable as the aphorism
that ends the "Ode on a Grecian Urn." My own view is that Lampman, like many Romantics at crucial moments in their work, means
what he says here, and that we err if we try to construe him in
some sense more congenial to twentieth-century biases. He neither
represses his knowledge of discord nor forgets the quotidian world
of experience and mortality; these things are acknowledged in the
sestet that ends his meditation. His endeavor in "The Frogs" is "to
estimate everything at its true value in relation to the universal and
the infinite."[8] This perspective approaches the noontide illumina-
tions of Eastern philosophy, which disdains the mutable world of
appearance; the speaker in "The Frogs" is "content to dream" even
as he realizes that destruction proceeds in another dimension. This
perspective also accords with Lampman's understanding of Keats,
for to be content that "dreams are real, and life is only sweet," is
to affirm a faith in "Beauty as comprehending all things that the
soul need care for." These affinities of vision suggest an explanation
for the speaker's shift from first-person singular to plural in the
concluding sonnet. "We" includes all his companions in such a
vision, even his reader, if the poem has worked its spell.

"Heat," which was written two months after "The Frogs," in
July 1887, has received more comment by far than any other Lamp-

man poem.[9] Perhaps this is because it is both utterly characteristic of Lampman and much less obviously indebted to models than many of his other works. In contrast to the rhetorical and allusive richness of "The Frogs" and "Among the Timothy," the language of "Heat" is brisk and direct, and its form is much less elaborate. The poem's central paradox is that the atmosphere of intense heat evoked is felt as liberating rather than as oppressive. This effect is due to both the lucidity of the verse and the sustained motif of liquidity that furnishes metaphors for the heat: "From plains that reel to southward, dim, / The road runs by me white and bare; / Up the steep hill it seems to swim / Beyond, and melt into the glare" (*PAL,* 12). The remarkable quality of this scene is its almost hallucinatory clarity. The literal hovers on the verge of a symbolic meaning, and forthwith this impressionistic landscape yields an emblem: an ascending hay-cart with its attendant wagoner. This bucolic figure might seem too slack to carry much symbolic freight, yet he is a fit representative of the kind of human aspiration that, beginning in nature, seeks to surmount without abusing or rejecting it. In a pairing that recurs in Lampman's work, the active laborer is a counterpart to the contemplative poet, who also harvests nature's bounty after his own fashion. At this point in the poem, the fate of this spiritual impulse in human nature is uncertain: the road merely "seems" to ascend to another dimension, and is lost in a harsh glare. The scene presages the epiphanic moment that eventually does arrive, in the fifth stanza.

The middle stanzas reinforce the sense of an ascending order through their vivid depiction of a hierarchy of living creatures—vegetable, insect, animal—culminating with the thrush whose song rises easily "into the pale depth of the noon" (*PAL,* 13). Unlike those more famous romantic birds, Keats's nightingale and Shelley's skylark, Lampman's thrush spans heaven and earth rather than evoking the traumatic sense of a gulf between. The thrush resembles the poet, who assimilates the hour to his own music, as the conclusion of the poem reveals:

> And yet to me not this or that
> Is always sharp or always sweet;
> In the sloped shadow of my hat
> I lean at rest, and drain the heat;
> Nay more, I think some blessèd power

> Hath brought me wandering idly here:
> In the full furnace of this hour
> My thoughts grow keen and clear.
>
> (*PAL,* 13)

This last stanza, culminating in a thought about thought, is meditative, and it presents a series of cruxes. Like most commentators
on the poem, I take "this or that" to refer to the two kinds of
consciousness mentioned at the opening of the preceding stanza:
"dreams," or the approach to visionary insight, and their "intervals"
of sensory alertness to outward things. There are times when dreams
fail to yield an illumination, just as there are times when sensuous
experience fails to yield delight. But in this instance they succeed,
for the speaker achieves a fertile equilibrium between passive sensitivity and creative action. At rest, he "drains" the heat: the verb
aptly expresses his active passivity, for it means more than the
dissipation of physical discomfort as he relaxes. Here it also means
"drink," as it does in the similar context of a later poem, "Comfort
of the Fields" (1889); the speaker is refreshed as he transmutes
phenomenal heat into spiritual light. With his next breath, he
acknowledges that such moments of insight involve more than an
act of will. They are mysteriously privileged, as are the works of
art that re-create them. It is appropriate, then, that the "thoughts"
of the final line mean not only his reflection upon "some blessèd
power," but also the symbolic ordering of details in the poem as a
whole.

The poet's acknowledgment that he does not always achieve a
relation to nature of such creative intensity suggests an epiphanic
experience; and indeed the Hesperian mood of the first four stanzas
yields to the epiphany of stanza five, where the language echoes the
Psalmist: "I will lift up mine eyes unto the hills, from whence
cometh my help" (Psalms 121:1). "Heat" is a splendid example of
Lampman's romantic re-vision of his Christian heritage. The "blessèd
power" on which he speculates in the final stanza is not the Lord,
but the same that Wordsworth evoked in the Simplon Pass episode
of *The Prelude*:

> Imagination—here the Power so called
> Through sad incompetence of human speech,
> That awful Power rose from the mind's abyss

Like an unfathered vapour that enwraps,
At once, some lonely traveller.
                    (1850, VI. 592–96)

The visionary experience that Lampman describes in "Heat" is less
exalted, more tempered by the relaxed style of a Hesperian consciousness. But like Wordsworth, he is a halted wayfarer whose
imagination finally transcends the light of sense. Just as the wagoner
of the opening stanzas becomes symbolic, so does the poet in the
final stanza, where he is identified with the figure of a pilgrim. He
is, however, a Romantic pilgrim, a wanderer who is not restricted
and directed to some particular shrine, but whose spiritual thirst
may be slaked anywhere in nature. Like the wisdom of the frogs,
the wisdom that he discovers is won without a quest.

Although "Heat" has proved more popular, "Among the Timothy" (1885) provides the finest synthesis of the motives and meth-
ods of Lampman's early nature poetry. In this complex meditation
the sensuous enjoyment of nature becomes intense, and the mellow
amplitude of a Hesperian sensibility is charged with epiphanic power.
In *Among the Millet,* the poem immediately follows "Heat," and it
also resembles that volume's much simpler title-piece: in each case,
the poet, at rest between earth and sky, fashions his dream in song.
Timothy is a meadow grass and only one of many details in a
landscape that furnishes the speaker with imagery of natural beauty
and vital process. The opening stanza, like the seed of any organism,
implies the ultimate form of the poem: a passage from bliss through
privation to renovation and contentment. It is at the same time an
eloquently simple description of a scene, and a landscape charged
with meaning; the Ontario countryside, and a meadow full of symbols. The metaphor in the first two lines humanizes time in the
figure of the morning, and introduces the pattern of loss, desire,
and gratification that anticipates the speaker's own experience as
the poem develops:

Long hours ago, while yet the morn was blithe,
   Nor sharp athirst had drunk the beaded dew,
A mower came, and swung his gleaming scythe
   Around this stump, and, shearing slowly, drew
Far round among the clover, ripe for hay,
      A circle clean and gray;
And here among the scented swathes that gleam,

> Mixed with dead daisies, it is sweet to lie
> And watch the grass and the few-clouded sky,
>   Nor think but only dream.
>
> (*PAL*, 13–14)

The mower introduces the theme of humanity's proper relation to nature: the harmonious and fruitful business of cultivation. The imaginative cultivation of nature is the poet's business, and in "Among the Timothy" the ground cleared by the mower becomes a magic circle for the speaker, who follows the haying with his own "crop of images and curious thoughts."[10] The dead and scattered flowers of this stanza will eventually be replaced by a vision of living daisies that accompanies a resurrection of the poet's spirit. The last line of the stanza introduces the distinction between thinking and dreaming that will evolve as the central theme of the poem.

The next two stanzas reveal the poet's motive for seeking comfort of the fields. He has passed from the confines of the city, his spirit parched like the morning hours at the outset of the poem, his distress exacerbated by the full heat of noon. This state of spiritual dryness, or dejection, is a major theme in romantic poetry. As M. H. Abrams has pointed out, dejection is the obverse of a cardinal Romantic value, hope, as well as the post-Christian version of a specific theological topic; just as in traditional Christian thought "sloth, accidie, had verged on the unredeemable sin of despair of grace, so in the Romantic view dejection breeds sterility, and to persist in a state of apathy and hopelessness is to live what Coleridge called a 'death-in-life.' "[11] Lampman's language evokes these ideas even as it persuades us that his experience of dejection is as deep as those that Wordsworth, Coleridge, and Shelley recorded in similar moments:

> And those high moods of mine that sometime made
>   My heart a heaven, opening like a flower
> A sweeter world where I in wonder strayed,
>   Begirt with shapes of beauty and the power
>   Of dreams that moved through that enchanted clime
>   With changing breaths of rhyme,
> Were all gone lifeless now, like those white leaves
>   That hang all winter, shivering dead and blind
>   Among the sinewy beeches in the wind,
>   That vainly calls and grieves.
>
> (*PAL*, 14)

This third stanza is the richest in the poem, and perhaps in all of Lampman's poetry. Even as he pursues the theme of loss and suffering, he gives us a magnificent picture of what he has lost: imagination, which on the terms he inherits from his precursors is the source of poetry itself. The central theme of Romanticism is that imagination can radically transform our relation to the common circumstances of human life. In "At the Mermaid Inn," 18 June 1892, Lampman made this high claim for the man who cultivates his awareness of natural beauty: "For him life is full of variety; every moment comes to him laden with some unique enjoyment, every hour is crowded with a multitude of fleeting but exquisite impressions . . . this serene source of satisfaction is in a greater or less degree within the reach of every man, if he will but accustom himself to the intelligent use of his senses" (*MI,* 94). This belief in an apocalypse of the here and now, an experience that makes the "heart a heaven," Lampman inherits from the English Romantics, who in turn adapted the theme from a writer whom Lampman's phrase may recall. At the end of *Paradise Lost* the archangel Michael comforts the exiled children of Eden with the promise that peace and happiness remain possible even in the fallen world: "then wilt thou not be loath / To leave this Paradise, but shalt possess / A paradise within thee, happier far" (XII. 585–87). Milton emphasizes the moral life, and the Romantics the imaginative life, as the opening to this paradise within. Lampman rarely uses the word "imagination," perhaps because he wished to avoid a term that was overworn by the late nineteenth century. However, his account in "Among the Timothy" of those "moods" of which he has been for the moment dispossessed, tallies in every detail with accounts of the imagination given in English Romantic poetry. The heart that opens "like a flower" affirms the organic principle in life and poetry. A sense of wonder is virtually a defining quality of imagination. The "shapes of beauty" moving through an "enchanted clime" recall the powerful figures that animate Romantic myth. And in the last part of this stanza Lampman expresses his spiritual desolation through a distinctively Romantic archetype of the imagination: the stricken leaves of beech trees that shudder in the grieving winter wind suggest a ruined Aeolian harp. Later in "Among the Timothy" Lampman presents an image of the harp restored as an emblem of his psychic recovery, completing the pattern that Abrams elucidated in a classic essay on "the correspondent breeze." Abrams observed that in Romantic poetry the image of a freshening breeze often replaces traditional invocations to a Muse, or to Apollo: "the wind becomes both the stimulus and outer correspondent to a spring-like revival of the spirit after a frozen wintry season, and also to a revival of poetic inspiration."[12] Lampman's retrieval of the root-meaning of "inspiration"—the association of wind with "changing breaths of rhyme"—is quite clear in this stanza as in several other of his poems. But at this point in "Among the Timothy," the wind is confined to a simile, and absent from the arid interior and exterior landscapes of the poet's consciousness.

The following stanza amplifies the distinction introduced in the opening stanza between thought and dream: the one faculty is properly a function of the other. "Dream," the comprehensive state of mind, includes emotional, aesthetic, and moral sensitivity as well as cerebral activity. When thought is properly harmonized with these other vital impulses, mind communes with nature, poetry and other arts become possible, and the heart is made a heaven. But when thought usurps consciousness—when the "overtaskèd brain" obliterates a subtler integrity of awareness—mind divides from nature, the dream evaporates, and the heart is made a sterile desert of dejection. Lampman's phrase, "unbournèd thought," expresses the mixed blessing of this special human faculty. Thought serves imagination when as a creative power it surpasses the limits of formal logic or ideology; but "unbournèd" also implies severance from the earth, and thought starves imagination when it forsakes the nourishment of natural things. However, this stanza marks the turning point in the poet's despair. His recourse is to renounce mental effort altogether, and let his perceptions wander: in this submission of mind to nature, and to its own free energies, his spiritual recovery and the revival of his creative power begins. This differs from the course of events in the principal poems of dejection written by his precursors. Coleridge, for example, only partially eases his sense of imaginative desolation in "Dejection: An Ode" through a vicarious enjoyment of the imaginative strength that survives in other people. Wordsworth, in the "Immortality Ode," accepts as permanent the loss of an intuitive sense of glory in the natural world, though he finds sufficient consolation in the wisdom that comes with age. In "Ode to Duty" Wordsworth seeks his rest from spiritual weariness through embracing an external code. Lampman was later to write his own version of an ode to duty in "Peccavi, Domine" (1894), but in "Among the Timothy" he discovers that the very act of abandoning mental effort brings about a fresh communion with nature.

In the ensuing stanzas the poet's surrender of willful purpose is reflected in the absence of personal reference as he notices details in the landscape. As in so many Romantic nature poems, a spiritual renewal is ushered in by gentle winds: here they toss the long timothy grass while "scarcely heeding" the little daisies rooted in the earth. These breezes, like the poet, are relaxed, and they whisper through the leaves of a lone poplar tree standing in the heat of the day. This last feature in the scene is, of course, the Aeolian harp of stanza three restored, an emblem of the poet inspired at intervals by the "correspondent breeze." Perhaps the words "leaves" and "beat" hint at the medium of poetry itself; indeed, these terms are followed by the purely poetic comparison of stirring poplar leaves to drowsy maenads, who in turn hint at the sexual factor in aroused creative energy. Other voices now take up the chorus of natural sounds—or at least now the poet notices them. His peripheral awareness of the continuing activity of mowers in the field recalls the theme of cultivation with which the poem began, and his imaginative harvest of the varied sights and sounds of the landscape parallels the actual harvest of mown hay.

The whole poem, like the seminal opening stanza, has moved from past to present tense, and it is the poet's total being-in-the-present that heals his spirit and gathers his several faculties—sensation, feeling, moral intuition, and the redeemed tyrant thought—into the ultimate reality of a waking dream. "Quite fashioned to forget," he eliminates only memory, the premise of a past tense, from this unity of consciousness. Lampman would have us understand that such dreams are the opposite of those that come with slumber. His dream among the timothy is not introverted but is, on the contrary, a kind of empathy: the ego vanishes as the mind absorbs and is absorbed into the natural landscape.

In the final stanza he stresses again that through this immersion in nature his visionary powers are renewed. The sense of time that attends this experience eludes our categories because it contains and resolves them. The intense moment of noon, now relished rather

than suffered, extends through the ongoing hours. The stasis of
epiphany suffuses the ripening of a Hesperian sense of process:

> And hour by hour among all shapes that grow
>   Of purple mints and daisies gemmed with gold
> In sweet unrest my visions come and go;
>   I feel and hear and with quiet eyes behold;
>   And hour by hour, the ever-journeying sun,
>   In gold and shadow spun,
> Into mine eyes and blood, and through the dim
>   Green glimmering forest of the grass shines down,
>   Till flower and blade, and every cranny brown,
>   And I are soaked with him.
>
> (PAL, 16)

This final image of a consciousness saturated with the sun's light
and heat appears in a number of Lampman's lyrics. Throughout this
poem, the emphasis has been on visual relaxation, with the subordination of sight in a revised proportion to taste (stanzas one,
five), smell (one), hearing (six, seven), and feeling (eight, nine).
Nevertheless, visual perception, symbolized by the sun, reasserts its
authority in the resolution of "Among the Timothy" and it remains
the dominant sense in Lampman's body of poetry. Its chief rival is
the sense of hearing, usually symbolized by the wind. These two
forces preside everywhere in Lampman's poems, in both contrary
and complementary relations. The visual is his passive sense, related
to his stoical proclivities and his temptation to regard nature merely
as a refuge. His auditory sense is related to his antipathy toward
Stoicism, and his confidence in the creative energies of imagination.
Generally, the wind is preaesthetic, associated with inspiration,
initiative, process, and discovery. The sun is primarily associated
with the aesthetic moment and with order, submission, stasis, and
revelation. Indeed, these are the roles assumed by sun and wind in
"Among the Timothy," which can be read as a lyrical drama per-
formed in the theater of poetic consciousness. A cruel sun dominates
the speaker's imaginative apathy in the opening stanzas but gives
way to gentle breezes that revive his spirit in the central part of the
poem. In the penultimate stanza, the two powers are in balance:
"To wind and sun and peaceful sound laid bare." And in the end
the dream is consummated in the union of consciousness with a sun
that has regained omnipotence, but become benign.

"Among the Timothy" is a superb poem and a worthy successor to the major English Romantic lyrics. In the end, however, it leaves us with the same question as Lampman's affirmation in "The Frogs," that "change and pain are shadows faint and fleet, / And dreams are real, and life is only sweet." Is the dream of art truly redemptive, and more than a source of strength and comfort, a solution to the problem of our divided lives? Ultimately, even "Among the Timothy" does not fully integrate the poet's knowledge of life and nature. The prolonged flood of sunshine at the poem's end only temporarily disperses the shadow that darkens many of his landscapes: his consciousness of himself and of other human lives. He excludes memory from his synthesis, and it is memory that endows us with two essentially human qualities, a sense of personal identity and a knowledge of death. His solitude (despite the distant harvesters in the scene) is equally significant. Human relations are all but absent from this vision, and sexuality wholly sublimated. The realities of ego, erotic desire, and personal mortality perplex and limit Lampman's landscapes of spiritual fulfillment. He was too good a poet, though, to avoid them altogether, and he acknowledges their stubborn presence at three points in the highly organized sequence of nature poems that constitutes his second published volume.

The Shifting Sun

The place of *Lyrics of Earth* in Lampman's development as a poet is a complex issue for several reasons. He found a publisher for the book only after several frustrating years of rejections, and only after its contents had been arbitrated by E. W. Thomson. [13] Of the twenty-nine poems it contains, all but three (and the dedication verses) had been completed by the end of 1892. The volume therefore represents Lampman's "nature work" in the years 1888 through 1892, following upon the publication of *Among the Millet*. Like the cycle of nature poems in that book, the lyrics in his second volume are arranged according to the seasons. While they also repeat other features of the earlier nature poetry, they are generally more naturalistic in method and more restrained in style. Several longer pieces, such as "Comfort of the Fields" (1889) and "The Meadow" (1890), suffer from that excessive "anatomy of description" that Coleridge warned against. Moreover, the mythopoeic richness of the earlier work is abated. In *Lyrics of Earth,* the nostalgic evocations of Arcadia indicate a diminution in the poet's visionary power, and his treatment of noontide confirms that loss. The image appears with greater frequency but with less intensity than it possesses in the three powerful landscape visions in *Among the Millet*. In these later lyrics, noontide has declined from an archetype to a convention, and lapsed from its status as a privileged time to its function as merely one among several phases that mark the sun's shifting course. Given these changes in Lampman's landscape vision, it is not surprising that the three outstanding poems in *Lyrics of Earth* concern the problematic aspects of vision itself.

It was Thomson who thought of placing "The Sweetness of Life" (1890) at the outset of *Lyrics of Earth,* a suggestion that Lampman accepted enthusiastically. In its memorable delineation of the poet's questioning approach to nature, it makes a fitting introduction to the volume. In some respects its atmosphere is reminiscent of the hot summer noonscape of "Heat," and it also reverberates with scriptural echoes, especially of the Psalms. The impressionistic method that generally shapes Lampman's nature poetry is absent. Unlike most of his nature poems, "The Sweetness of Life" was composed out of season, probably in December 1890; like "A Vision of April" (1895), an important later poem also composed out of season, it has the symbolic intensity of a parable.

Scriptural traces haunt the opening stanza, but there is no sign here or in what follows of the fearful Presence that inspired the Psalmist's praise and supplication. In the end we encounter an apparition, but it is of another, diminished order than those of Old Testament prophecy. Meanwhile, the poet assumes a quintessentially Romantic stance as he questions the things of nature, in which he sees mirrored the mystery of his own condition. His ostensible theme is happiness, but the poem has a melancholy undertone even in its opening line, with the suggestion of an inexplicable randomness in human life. As in the opening stanzas of "The Frogs" and "Heat," here again the word "seem" registers an uncertain note, raising the Romantic poet's persistent doubt about the life and sympathy he attributes to the natural world.

Through the next two stanzas, the meadow, flowers, and brook answer him in chorus, and the landscape becomes vividly symbolic:

> What sayst thou, O meadow,
>   That stretchest so wide, so far,

> That none can say how many
>   Thy misty marguerites are?
> And what say ye, red roses,
>   That o'er the sun-blanched wall
> From your high black-shadowed trellis
>   Like flame or blood-drops fall?
>   (*PAL*, 125)

The crucial meaning in this scene is implied in the contrast between its background and foreground. The meadow suggests an infinite profusion of life and beauty, a prodigality that baffles understanding. (In plant lore, the field of daisies or marguerites is associated with St. Augustine's vision of the spirits of the blessed.) From this vista of distance, scope, and possibility, we are brought up sharply by the roses, which confront us with elemental facts and limits. The roses, brilliant against their dark background, present a wonderful image of life or passion, which splendidly consumes itself. There is a hint of violence here, but it is subdued to a stronger sense of beauty. The sweetness of life is a function of its very brevity and mystery. This bitter-sweet understanding is given in more explicit terms in the refrain, which also follows this third stanza:

> What sayest thou, O shadow,
>   That from the dreaming hill
> All down the broadening valley
>   Liest so sharp and still?
> And thou, O murmuring brooklet,
>   Whereby in the noonday gleam
> The loosestrife burns like ruby,
>   And the branchèd asters dream?
>   "We are born, we are reared, and we linger
>   A various space and die;
>   We dream and are very happy,
>   But we cannot answer why."
>   (*PAL*, 125–26)

Here at once are the valley of the shadow of death, and the stream of life and utterance that discovers its utmost fulfillment in a noon-day epiphany. This scene has the same clarity as the landscape of "Heat," but the epiphany here lacks the transforming power of the expansive noontide visions in *Among the Millet*. The word "gleam" connotes inconstancy, brevity, and illusion. A gleam is reflected

light, and the poet's vision fails in this instance to penetrate beyond
a world of appearances that only mirror his mortality and finite
understanding.

In the final stanza, the poet's awareness of mortality becomes
personal in a beautifully simple expression of self-consciousness. His
knowledge echoes the Psalmist: "*As for* man, his days *are* as grass:
as a flower of the field, so he flourisheth. For the wind passeth over
it, and it is gone; and the place thereof shall know it no more"
(Psalms 103: 15–16). As a Romantic—and a modern—Lampman
lacks the Psalmist's consolation. The only spiritual presence he can
address is of his own imagining: dubiously supernatural, and vaguely
disquieting:

> And then of myself I questioned,
>   That like a ghost the while
> Stood from me and calmly answered,
>   With slow and curious smile:
> "Thou art born as the flowers, and wilt linger
>   Thine own short space and die;
> Thou dream'st and art strangely happy,
>   But thou canst not answer why."
>
> (*PAL,* 126)

This enigmatic ghost is the poet's introspective self, a descendant
of Blake's Spectres, Shelley's "Alastor," and the self-projected phantoms that torment Byron's hero in "Manfred"—all expressions of
the lethal solipsism that imperils the Romantic quest for self-ful-
fillment. Lampman's specter is not nearly as menacing as the kindred
figures in his precursors. His self-consciousness here is a voluntary
state that can be resolved again into unity of being. "Dreaming"
remains for him a more integrated form of awareness than the analytical mind that questions hot after certainties; he insists again
and again that the common world of routine, doubt, and care is
merely shadow, and that the world of imagination is what is ultimately real and substantial. Nevertheless, his curiously smiling
ghost is strangely compelling, and a subversive figure in his realm
of dreams.

Spectral imagery is typical of Lampman's Autumn poems and of
particular importance in one of the key lyrics of earth. "In November" (1889) seems to have been designed as an ironic contrary to

"Among the Timothy," so deliberate is its pattern of contrast. Wandering in the woods on a bleak November day, the speaker finds "a clearing, where the broken ground / Was scattered with black stumps and briers" (*PAL*, 158–59). Like the circle of grass mown round the stump in "Among the Timothy," this clearing is magic ground, but it is signed with very different forces: the "old wreck of forest fires" and the withered stalks of mulleins. It is implicitly a blasted heath, resembling such landscapes of blighted quest as those of Browning's "Childe Roland" and T. S. Eliot's *Waste Land*. The scores of dead mulleins in the clearing draw the speaker's special notice:

> Not plants at all they seemed to me,
> But rather some spare company
> Of hermit folk, who long ago,
> Wandering in bodies to and fro,
> Had chanced upon this lonely way,
> And rested thus, till death one day
> Surprised them at their compline prayer,
> And left them standing lifeless there.
>
> (*PAL*, 159)

This is a remarkable passage, not least because of the paradox inherent in a "company" of hermits. The lines are certainly open to diverse interpretations; my view is that these mullein-hermits represent Romantic nature-poets whose reclusive worship estranges them from one another and is ironically confuted by death. The speaker's affinity with this scene has consequences startlingly different from his immersion in the landscape of "Among the Timothy." As at the climax of the earlier poem, his ego vanishes as he is absorbed into the scene:

> I stood
> Among the mullein-stalks as still
> As if myself had grown to be
> One of their sombre company,
> A body without wish or will.
>
> (*PAL*, 159)

Far from bringing on a resurrection, the assimilation of self to nature renders him a living corpse: what he discovers in these woods is a

foreshadowing of his death. But the epiphany of the poem is yet to
come. It is initiated, as we might expect, by a soft wind and a shaft
of sunlight through the clouds. The transfiguration of landscape is,
however, curiously qualified. There is something sinister in the
wind's "secret stir" as well as in the quality of the sunshine. This
nebulous transfiguration is only a dim likeness of "some former
dream"—the triumphant vision of "Among the Timothy," for example. Nor are such prior achievements helpful now: as Browning's
Childe Roland also discovered, the Wordsworthian resort to memory
of epiphanies past is of no avail in the present crisis. The Romantic
moment of "In November" is assessed in terms that exactly reverse
the value that Lampman elsewhere claims for such experiences. Here
it is the epiphany rather than ordinary consciousness that is represented as shadowy and unreal, though it does serve to release him
from his deathlike trance:

> And I, too, standing idly there,
> With muffled hands in the chill air,
> Felt the warm glow about my feet,
> And shuddering betwixt cold and heat,
> Drew my thoughts closer, like a cloak,
> While something in my blood awoke,
> A nameless and unnatural cheer,
> A pleasure secret and austere.
>
> (PAL, 160)

What he recovers is an awareness of his human life distinct from
the landscape: his feeling is "unnatural" because of this sense of his
separation as a thinking creature from the shriveled vegetation in
the clearing. In view of the critique of thinking in "Among the
Timothy," it is significant that here thought guards him from an
inhospitable natural environment. There is an integration of perception, feeling, and thought in the resolution of this poem, but
it is a strictly interior harmony that depends on an estrangement
from nature. The form of "In November" also contrasts with the
eddying rhythms and structure of "Among the Timothy." Its regular
procession of couplets and the direct reportage of events suggest a
normal sense of duration, even of measured time, though here such
linear order is valued rather than feared: the steady verse-rhythms
provide a ritual charm against the menacing elements in the landscape.

I am not arguing that "In November" should be taken for a wholesale repudiation by Lampman of his visionary nature poetry. It is immediately followed in *Lyrics of Earth* by another Autumn poem in which withered mulleins appear as images of seasonal beauty rather than as spectral presences, and in which a shaft of sunlight stimulates a renewed sense of identity with landscape. Still, like "The Sweetness of Life," "In November" strikes a contrary note in *Lyrics of Earth,* and this counterpoint of doubt is consummated in the long poem that Lampman originally intended for the final piece in the volume.

"Winter-Store" is the kind of poem that yields its full meaning only in the light of its author's whole body of work, and perhaps only in the wider light of the tradition in which his poetry participates. Moreover, to appreciate its significance for Lampman, we need to know something about the circumstances of its composition and publication. Although it was published as the second-last poem in *Lyrics of Earth,* it had been intended by Lampman to conclude the volume: he inserted "The Sun Cup" (c. 1888–89) at the end only upon finding that his publisher's proofs had omitted this short lyric from its proper place earlier in the sequence. "Winter-Store" consists of three movements of 34, 158, and 44 lines. These reflect the poem's piecemeal composition from about 1887 to 1893, and their evolution reveals a transformation in Lampman's thinking during that period. His manuscripts show that he first composed the middle section, and that the earliest lines, on the delights of a noonday ramble through a summer landscape, were written at about the same time as "Heat," around July 1887. A fair copy dated December 1889 represents a tentatively complete version that Lampman later deemed inadequate. This draft has a variant opening, much lighter in tone, and it wholly omits the troubled ending of the poem as eventually published. The three stanzas that Lampman subsequently made the introductory movement were composed around January 1892 and published as an independent poem, "Vision," in November that year.[14] The two stanzas that he added as the closing movement were written at about the latter date, and the final version of "Winter-Store" was organized sometime between late 1892 and the submission of Lampman's manuscript to Copeland and Day in 1895.

The introductory movement is a little "crisis poem" complete in itself, but unusual in its use of the first person plural. The opening

lines exhort a typically Romantic refinement of vision: "subtly conscious, all awake," we may "see the wonder as it is" (*PAL,* 165).
But this desirable relation to nature is suddenly lost: "turned sharply
inward," we suffer the atrophy of visionary power and a lapse into
the apathy familiar in Romantic dejection poems. The prologue
ends, however, with a reaffirmation of faith that, despite the common blindness of humanity, individuals may still recover their lapsed
vision.

D. M. R. Bentley has suggested that the opening lines of "Winter-Store" were inspired by Wordsworth's "Immortality Ode," as
they describe how the visionary strength of childhood is attenuated
by experience.[15] I not only consider this probable, but also think
that Lampman alludes—consciously or not—to two other English
Romantic poems in this prologue. His accusation that by and large
we are oblivious to "the magic pageantry, . . . issuing in perpetual
change / From the rainbow gates of Time" employs one of Shelley's
major symbols, the most celebrated context of which is "Adonais":
"Life, like a dome of many-coloured glass, / Stains the white radiance
of Eternity . . ." ("Adonais," 462–63). Shelley's elegy resembles
the "Immortality Ode" in its vision of birth and experience as an
"eclipsing Curse" (480). It is then appropriate that Lampman's third
allusion is to the poet for whom "Adonais" was written. The lines,
"Nature from her holy place, / Bending with unveilèd face," recall
the figure of Moneta in "The Fall of Hyperion." Keats's "High
Prophetess" is, of course, no incarnation of Nature. My reasons for
believing this an allusion appear below; here I want to emphasize
that in "Winter-Store" Lampman confronts a crucial problem in his
vision of nature, and that therefore it should not be surprising that
he echoes three poems that marked spiritual crises in the lives of
the poets who influenced him most.

Lampman's prologue is delivered in the impersonal "we," and
resolved with the affirmation that "he who . . . knows the great
and fair" can recover oneness with nature and visionary joy. In the
long middle section of "Winter-Store" the poet shifts to the first
person singular in a detailed prospect of just such a communion
with landscape: "Up the fielded slopes at morn, / Where light wefts
of shadow pass, / Films upon the bending corn, / I shall sweep the
purple grass" (*PAL,* 166). What follows is a cornucopia of delightful
sights and sounds, a virtual inventory of the imagery that pervades
Lampman's nature poetry. Read on its own merits, this part of

"Winter-Store" may seem overlong, superficial, too much of a mere list. Read with Lampman's other landscapes in mind, such images as sun, wind, stream, frogs, and choruses of insects acquire rich significance. As usual, the speaker is for the most part alone, in "outer solitudes" and beside secret forest brooks. He passes from seeing and hearing to the familiar consummation: "I shall dream by upland fences" (*PAL,* 169). He also moves from morning to an extended noontide reminiscent of "Heat" and "Among the Timothy," but eventually this diurnal pattern gives way to an awareness of seasonal change. Presently it is autumn and he considers the bleak months to come, taking comfort in his store of abundant images. Having harvested his spiritual nourishment, he feels secure against the onset of winter:

> When the high Aurora gleams
> Far above the Arctic streams
> Like a line of shifting spears,
> And the broad pine-circled meres,
> Glimmering in that spectral light,
> Thunder through the northern night;
> Then within the bolted door
> I shall con my summer store;
> Though the fences scarcely show
> Black above the drifted snow,
> Though the icy sweeping wind
> Whistle in the empty tree,
> Safe within the sheltered mind,
> I shall feed on memory.
>
> (*PAL,* 171)

There are several notable things in this passage, which closes the second part of the poem. The idea of winter as mocker and the parodied Aeolian harp as a symbol of imaginative inertness are details familiar from poems in *Among the Millet.* Contrary to Lampman's other winter poems, here there is no reconciliation with the season; it is envisaged as a purely alien and fearful time. The lines on the Northern Lights are especially striking. Byron made use of the image in *Don Juan* (VII. 1–2) but Lampman's lines put me in mind of those written fifty years later by Wallace Stevens, in "The Auroras of Autumn": "The scholar of one candle sees / An Arctic effulgence flaring on the frame / Of everything he is. And he feels afraid."

Writing on Stevens, Harold Bloom claims that the Northern Lights "confront the poet with an inhuman imagination, a sublime that appalls . . . their splendor confronts the poet with the challenge and fear of a total questioning of the capability of human imagination to match the power of reality."[16]

Such a meaning might seem irrelevant to Lampman had he chosen—as he first planned—to end "Winter-Store" within a sheltered mind, feeding on memories of summer. But in the finally written, final movement of the poem, he does an astonishing volteface: his winter-store, the forms of memory, are scattered by a vision of the social landscape, and what follows is an inventory of human life in its disturbing miscellany of hope and despair, joy and grief, innocence and corruption. Like Keats in "The Fall of Hyperion," Lampman faces a devastating challenge to his dreams: the knowledge of "those to whom the miseries of the world / Are misery, and will not let them rest" (I. 148–49). These lines are spoken by Moneta, who represents a reality-principle that insists that the poet admit all facets of the human condition, its glory and its darkness alike. Since she also presides over Keats's farewell to pastoral poetry, there is considerable irony in Lampman's use of her as a model for the benign figure of Nature in the first section of "Winter-Store." At the end of this poem the speaker's awareness of human suffering impairs his sense of natural beauty, reversing his previous state of mind. Discovering his identity with humanity and acknowledging his share in its passion and sorrow, Lampman, like Keats, relinquishes his belief in dreams and his inclination toward pastoral:

> All these sleep, and through the night,
> Comes a passion and a cry,
> With a blind sorrow and a might,
> I know not whence, I know not why,
> A something I cannot control,
> A nameless hunger of the soul.
> It holds me fast. In vain, in vain,
> I remember how of old
> I saw the ruddy race of men,
> Through the glittering world outrolled,
> A gay-smiling multitude,
> All immortal, all divine,
> Treading in a wreathèd line
> By a pathway through a wood.
>
> (PAL, 172–73)

This is one of the most memorable moments in Lampman's poetry. The vision of an Arcadian race remains compelling despite his vision of men as they are; still, the loss of a deep faith is the burden of his poem. It is a Romantic palinode equaled in its poignancy only by Wordsworth's "Elegiac Stanzas."

While "Winter-Store" lacks the technical brilliance and density of "Among the Timothy," it stands as the major poem of Lampman's second volume. As a catalog in tetrameter couplets, it resembles "L'Allegro" and "Il Penseroso," but apart from one or two phrases the similarity to Milton's lyrics ends there. Although Lampman's poem begins with an impersonal prologue, it becomes one of his most moving personal statements. It reflects his understanding of three seminal poems by the English Romantics, and it expresses a fundamental change in his own poetic vision. Specifically, it is an admission of the limitations of his central mode of poetry, the Romantic nature lyric. He became dissatisfied with the genre as he came to realize that the imagination is a human, not a natural phenomenon, and a mixed blessing with a darker side than his landscape poetry could express. Hence the more human contexts of his dreams: the city, and erotic love.

Chapter Five
The Apocalyptic City
Poetry and Society

Lampman's companionship with nature was not enough. He found comfort and inspiration in the fields, but no lasting solvent for an insistent social conscience and a need for love. When he wrote to E. W. Thomson in October 1893 that his third volume of poems was to be "less description, more human life" (*CLT,* 94), he indicated a genuine shift in the character of his poetry. He had written poems of "human life" since the early eighties and would continue to produce nature poems until he died, but the former increased in proportion and significance through the nineties. Lampman was heir to a century of profound social change and intense political controversy, and as a civil servant in his nation's capital he was an eyewitness to misgovernment and corruption. It is little wonder, then, that he wrote many poems that have a political meaning more or less explicit depending on their form.[1]

The tension between an autonomous art and a sense of social responsibility is a hallmark of nineteenth-century poetry. The English Romantics tried to resolve this tension in various ways, characteristically in the idea that poets are prophets who serve humanity through their special capacity to express spiritual realities. In Shelley's famous phrase, "poets are the unacknowledged legislators of the World."[2] But as they evolved their personal mythologies out of the disintegrating public myths of the past, the Romantics tended to isolate themselves, and their art, from the society that they wished to influence. Lampman nowhere shows himself so truly their heir as in his awareness of this dilemma, which is usually the theme of his poems about poetry: "Why do ye call the poet lonely, / Because he dreams in lonely places? / He is not desolate, but only / Sees, where ye cannot, hidden faces" (*PAL,* 11). This little verse of 1884 could be an epigram by Blake. ("Great things are done when Men & Mountains meet. / This is not done by Jostling in the Street."[3]) Here Lampman anticipates the criticism that he was to receive as a

86

nature poet, and replies by affirming the superior insight of the prophetic writer. Undoubtedly, the poet's "dreams" would include nature lyrics of the sort that dominate Lampman's first two volumes; the "faces" that he sees might be the mythopoeic figures that emerge, especially in his seasons poems, to humanize the landscape. But I take Lampman's epigram to be a quarrel with himself as much as rhetoric for unappreciative readers: he registers here an inner debate about the ultimate value of an art that minimizes social realities.

The relation of the poet to his community is also the theme of two longish poems by Lampman that are similar in form but rather different in their perceptions. "The Poet's Song" (1890) depicts the Poet as an heroic figure opposed to a moribund society. Part I, written in modified sapphics, describes a kingdom blighted by a drought that symbolizes the people's spiritual desolation. The sterile cycles of palace routine contrast with the life-renewing seasonal cycles in Lampman's nature poetry, an antithesis that also appears in his best poem in the prophetic mode, "The City of the End of Things." The title figure of "The Poet's Song," who shares in the general dearth of creativity, sits with his broken lute and listlessly marks the dull passing of time: "He saw the midnight bright and bare / Fill with its quietude of stars / The silence that no human prayer / Attains or mars" (*PAL*, 211–12). This is a curious stanza; even as he pictures a universe void of Deity, Lampman evokes pre-Copernican notions of an unsullied firmament and sublunary corruption. "The Poet's Song" combines the traditional symbolism of prophetic literature with a bitterness that is perhaps rather more personal than archetypal: it may be worth noting that this poem recasts as a narrative essentially the same experience that "Among the Timothy" treats as a subjective crisis. When the stricken Poet overhears a woman's laughter, he curses, mocked in his own barrenness by the sound of erotic delight. When a messenger bids him attend the king, he refuses in metaphors that were commonplaces for the poetic process among the Romantic poets: "The tree is perished to its root, / The fountain dry" (*PAL*, 213). Part II describes a change in these conditions and accordingly changes to another stanza form, as a "correspondent breeze" ushers in a storm that revives the Poet's creative energy. The poem's conclusion will probably remind us of Gray or Collins rather than any of the major Romantics except perhaps Blake, whose prophecies are partly rooted in the bardic tradition of the mid-eighteenth century. Lampman's archetypal Poet abandons a decayed civilization of tyrant and slaves to rediscover the sublime features of the enduring natural world and to chant his music above the mountain gorges. The presence of shepherds who bear witness to this birth of creative power implies that the Poet is a type of Christ, incarnation of the divine energies that will redeem individuals from the collapse of the old order.

Six years later, in "The Minstrel" (1896), Lampman took a more problematic view of the poet's relation to society. This work, written in true sapphics, resembles the "progress" poems of the eighteenth century, but is thoroughly post-Romantic in its vision.[4] The title figure again represents poets in general, but here Lampman adds a historical perspective to the archetypal fabling of "The Poet's Song." The first half of the poem describes the Minstrel's activities during the course of a day; what the details imply, however, is a history of English poetry from its beginnings to the present. The second and third stanzas approximate the style of Old English verse, as the Minstrel chronicles battles and celebrates their heroes. After passing from these subjects to the chivalric themes of hunting and love, the historical pattern disappears for several stanzas. The emphasis remains, however, on the continuity and cohesion of a community in which the Minstrel plays a vital role through fostering social ritual, domestic affection, and religious conviction. Then, in the pivotal stanzas, the historical allegory reappears. At this point the poet ceases to be an integral member of his society, and becomes an isolated seer. The subject of this passage is, of course, the advent of Romanticism:

> So the minstrel sang with a hundred voices
> All day long, and now in the dusk of even
> Once again the gates of the city opened,
> > Wide for his passing
>
> Forth to dreaming meadows, and fields, and wooded
> Hillsides, solemn under the dew and the starlight. . . .
> > > > (PAL, 306–7)

This is the familiar landscape of Lampman's nature poetry. The meadows and fields reflect the poet's own state of mind as he spins his solitary dream into a vision of great beauty, a "song for the spirit only": "Sorrow touched it, travail of spirit, broken / Hopes, and faiths uprooted, and aspirations / Dimmed and soiled, and out of the depth of being / Limitless hunger" (*PAL,* 307). This is a brilliantly condensed view of the primary motives of Romantic poetry. The remaining stanzas resume the progress form but instead of a general history of poetry, the Minstrel presents a quintessentially Romantic theme: the history of the individual artist's development. He proceeds from personal expression, through an articulation of the human condition of uncertainty and grief, to a religious vision that reads the cosmos as God's script. But this last is emphatically a private vision, achieved only once:

> —for just as the solemn glory,
> Flung by the moonshine,
>
> Over folds of hurrying clouds at midnight,
> Gleams and passes, so was his song—the noblest—
> Once outpoured, and then in the strain and tumult
> Gone and forgotten.
>
> (*PAL,* 308)

This view of the transience and inconsequence of art exceeds the pessimism of the English Romantics in their most dejected moments. The moving quality of these lines is their serenity. The heroic attitude of the isolated bard at the end of "The Poet's Song" seems like posturing beside this deeply tragic sense of the Minstrel's estrangement from his community.

A Political Vision

"The Minstrel" is a relatively late work in Lampman's career. By and large, he was, like his major precursors, more inclined to seek ways of reaffirming the uses of poetry. As a post-Christian visionary literature, Romantic poetry is redemptive in its general bearing, though specific conceptions of redemption may vary with different writers and at different times in the careers of individuals. At first Lampman sought his redemption through an imaginative response to nature, but gradually his sense of the limitations of nature poetry combined with his moral idealism to stimulate his interest in concepts of social redemption.

The English Romantics patterned their redemptive visions after the apocalyptic passages of the Bible. As M. H. Abrams has shown, the course of events set in motion by the French Revolution first raised, then shattered the hopes of Blake, Wordsworth, and Coleridge for the arrival of the millennium. Their faith in an "apocalypse by revolution" was eventually replaced by the idea that personal redemption could be achieved through imaginative vitality—a view also developed in the next generation, in the poetry of Shelley.[5] Lampman clearly understood the crucial significance of the French Revolution for Shelley, Wordsworth, and Coleridge, as indeed for the Romantic movement as a whole.[6] His distance from them in time, however, with the intervention of substantial political reform and of interpretations of history fostered by Hegel, Darwin, and Marx, gave him a broader confidence in social change than the English Romantics had sustained through the collapse of the Revolution and the ascendancy of repressive British administrations during the first quarter of the nineteenth century. Lampman shared the exhilaration of the revolutionary phase of the English Romantics without sharing their disillusionment. His comments on their art also suggest his relation to Romantic politics:

They were like youthful Titans casting off from themselves magnificently the sordid conventions, false rules and fettering theories forged in the growth of two benighted centuries. They trod the earth like gods, and their foreheads touched the stars. It is the prime glory of the poetry of Shelley that it has given us the fullest expression of that wild and promethean spirit. Already in 1830 or 1840, when Tennyson and Browning came, this golden effervescence had nearly passed away, and men were settling down to the long task of sifting the chaotic ideas of their predecessors, and perfecting what there was in them of true and permanent through the application of clear and happy intelligence and devoted art.[7]

Lampman considered his own political idealism an inheritance from the Romantics to be employed in the critical spirit of more recent times. And indeed, his political poetry shows precisely a mixture—not always a synthesis—of Romantic and Victorian elements.

The English Romantics had been bred in polemics over the relation of people to sovereign. During the nineteenth century, controversy shifted to questions of political economy and to the social injustices that accompanied industrialization. In "Liberty" (1898), which takes as its title the political watchword of Romantic poetry, Lampman assessed the progress of social justice as the century drew toward its close. This poem opens with recollections of French

Revolutionary fervor and of the apocalyptic hope engendered in the early days of the revolt. The emphasis throughout is on language:

> Freedom, Ah! the cry
> Was a sword to conquer by
> Hate, injustice, tyranny
> Beneath the word would cease:
> Plenty, brotherhood, and peace
> Like a heaven for the free!
>
> (*ALS,* 28)

Words (as Lampman suggests) are the matrix of human freedom but also—especially as abstractions—the instruments of self-deception. Revolutionary slogans have their uses, but social transformation is not to be achieved by fiat. The use and abuse of language is a recurring theme in Lampman's work, and made most explicit in the sonnet "Fair Speech" (1889). In "Liberty" he presents a rapid survey of European history in the nineteenth century: the subordination of kings, the consolidation of nation states, the great increase of populations, cities, and material splendor. Misery and insecurity, however, remain the common lot, and oppression flourishes. Words such as "democracy" and "republic" have been perverted to sanction tyrannies as oppressive as the old monarchies, for tyranny persists, in Lampman's view, wherever unequal economic power makes the wills of men unequal. He illustrates this principle in a remarkable stanza that imaginatively recasts the imagery of one of the greatest of political lyrics, Blake's "London":

> Lo! the master still
> From his palace gate commands,
> And the toiler works his will
> With his worn and bleeding hands.
> Golden ladies sigh
> From their cushions and their lace,
> While the stricken trull goes by
> With her wild and haunted face.
>
> (*ALS,* 29)

Like Blake, Lampman focuses his arraignment of economic inequity on the corruption of human sexuality. The "golden" wives of the masters are as surely bought as the impoverished prostitute; liberty is the necessary but absent condition for love. The poem develops its indictment of capitalism as polarizing the population into classes that are equal only in their moral abasement. The rich feed their pride with power and luxury while the poor suffer a spiritual atrophy even more horrifying than their material circumstances. Was it for this, the poet asks rhetorically, that monarchies were curtailed? The concluding lines of "Liberty" insist that the revolutionary vision, albeit disappointed during the era of Robespierre and Napoleon, endures. Lampman implies that a widened understanding of history and injustice will finally bring about the millennium. How this proletarian enlightenment is to come about, and whether or not violence will be necessary, are left open questions. As usual, Lampman's technique complements his theme. The irregular stanzas of mixed quatrains and couplets, trimeters and tetrameters, anapests and trochees, suggest the struggle toward an emerging order, and create a tone of indignation and militant resolve.

The cosmopolitan point of view in "Liberty" is characteristic of Lampman's political lyrics: they contain virtually nothing that reflects his view of events in Ottawa or of issues particular to the Canadian society of his day. This was through choice rather than indifference. His "Mermaid Inn" columns and his letters are full of informed comment on current affairs, and denunciations of Parliament as "the national collection of cut-purses & bunco-men gathering together here."[8] They also show that he was concerned with nurturing national excellence through public education and the encouragement of art and literature, while at the same time he scorned the kind of mindless nationalism that he found in some of his contemporaries. On the publication of one of Charles G. D. Roberts's "patriotic outbursts," Lampman remarked that "the times can hardly carry patriotic verse, particularly of a boastful character. Satire would appear to be the species of verse most applicable to the present emergency" (MI, 19 November 1892, 194). Lampman himself had no real gift for satire and accordingly focused his political poetry on fundamental values rather than specific occasions. The only remotely topical piece among his political poems is "Crete" (1896), his sequence of three sonnets rebuking Western nations for their tardiness in aiding the revolt of the Christians on Crete against Turkish rule. And while these sonnets were inspired by a contemporary situation, as a prophecy of political liberty they extend the tradition of such other "occasional" poems as Blake's French Revo-

lution, Wordsworth's patriotic sonnets of 1802, and Shelley's "Hellas."

Liberty is the cardinal political value for Lampman, but finally indivisible from equality and justice: all are the condition for each. Some of his poems are parables that illustrate this principle. One of these, "Abu Midjan" (1885), is based on a story that he found in Simon Ockley's *History of the Saracens.* This poem tells of a Moslem warrior who remains chained to a tree, disgraced for drunkenness, while his emir's army engages the Persian host. He persuades the emir's wife to free him, promising to return to his chains after the battle, and outfitted with her husband's horse and armor, leads "the faithful" to victory. When the Emir Saad later describes to his wife the arrival on the field of his mysterious double, she tells him about the drunkard's promise: "To the garden went the Emir, / Running to the tree, and found / Torn with many wounds and bleeding, / Abu Midjan meek and bound" (*PAL,* 56). This is a crucifixion image, a Christian symbol employed to universalize the theme of the individual's relation to his community. Saad frees the prisoner, promising never again to punish him for taking wine, whereupon he replies: " 'While an earthly lord controlled me, / All things for the wine I bore; / Now since God alone doth judge me, / Abu Midjan drinks no more.' " (*PAL,* 57). When Desmond Pacey disparaged "Abu Midjan" as "a Victorian temperance tract," he missed its point.[9] Whatever we may think of the poem's technique, its meaning is not that abstinence is necessarily praiseworthy, but that a covenant renders individuals more valuable to their society than coercion. In his freedom, Abu Midjan is implicitly equal to Saad, as is symbolized in his assuming the emir's guise during the battle. More than a decade later, Lampman wrote a similar parable, "King Oswald's Feast" (1896), about a legendary ruler of Northumbria who is moved by news of his people's misery to distribute his food and riches among them. In this case king becomes commoner, reversing the pattern of "Abu Midjan" but illustrating the same relationship between liberty, equality, and justice. And again the figure of Christ is evoked not as a personal saviour but as a persecuted agent of social justice—indeed, a prototypical socialist.

Lampman believed socialism to be the one political system consistent with an active conscience. As F. W. Watt has pointed out, he was also the only Canadian poet of stature with close ties to Canadian radicalism in its earliest years.[10] His obituary in the *Ottawa*

Journal stressed his membership in the Social Science Club and the Fabian Society of Ottawa, and Duncan Campbell Scott also pointed out Lampman's commitment to socialist principles in his sketch for the memorial edition of *The Poems*.[11] More recently, Barrie Davies has edited an "untitled essay on socialism . . . a draft rather than a finished piece," which he suggests that Lampman wrote at a time when he was participating in informal political discussions.[12] As rough and brief as it is, this essay throws light on Lampman's basic position. His socialism is clearly an expression of moral vision rather than rationalist ideology, and rooted in Victorian idealism rather than in dialectical materialism:

The cause of socialism is the cause of love and hope and humanity: the cause of competition is the cause of anarchy, pessimism, and a disbelief in a possible Manhood for human nature just emerging from its barbarous infancy. The human soul is the highest thing of which we have any knowledge. If this soul is incapable of adapting itself to conditions of equality, community and brotherhood, then better had we never have been born, for reason, the capacity for faith was given to us in vain.[13]

Though at one or two points Lampman seems to echo Marx on the dynamics of class struggle, most of the essay is given over to arguing that history is moved by ideas and shaped by men of inspiration. Indeed, his second paragraph attacks a merely scientific approach to social questions; in his view, analyses that disregard human values—statements of economic "law," for example—offer only a partial and distorted perspective on society. Lampman's interpretation of history as showing "human nature just emerging from its barbarous infancy" corresponds to the evolutionary idealism of such poems as "The Clearer Self" (1894) and "The Largest Life" (1894–97). Also worth noting are the uncompromising tone of his argument and the ominous "if" that anticipates despair should his faith prove vain. In other moments, Lampman was to create poetry out of such despair. This essay, however, concludes with optimism that the barbarities that wrecked the French Revolution are a thing of the past, and that social change will now proceed "gradually and intelligently from possibility to possibility."

Lampman regarded socialism not as end in itself, but rather as promising a milieu wherein all individuals might have sufficient scope for personal fulfillment. Throughout his work he affirms an ideal of self-cultivation. His "Mermaid Inn" columns often deal with a theme that he took up again in his essay on "Happiness": the idea that everyone has an inborn gift that is the proper basis of one's character and vocation. Lampman emphasizes both the importance of nurturing such a "bent" in childhood and the danger of "mental or moral ruin" should it be neglected or suppressed. [14] His essays on this subject read like so many commentaries on his sonnet "Salvation" (1894):

> Nature hath fixed in each man's life for dower
> One root-like gift, one primal energy,
> Wherefrom the soul takes growth, as grows a tree,
> With sap and fibre, branch and leaf and flower;
> But if this seed in its creative hour
> Be crushed and stifled, only then the shell
> Lifts like a phantom falsely visible,
> Wherein is neither growth, nor joy, nor power.
> Find thou this germ, and find thou thus thyself,
> This one clear meaning of the deathless I,
> This bent, this work, this duty—for thereby
> God numbers thee, and marks thee for His own:
> Careless of hurt, or threat, or praise, or pelf,
> Find it and follow it, this, and this alone!
>
> (*PAL,* 263–64)

The notion of the human mind as a plant that fulfills its potential through proper nourishment and spontaneous growth is a familiar Romantic metaphor. In extending this metaphor to the "soul," Lampman suggests that the true spiritual form of each individual is inherent, not contingent on circumstances. Genuine identity— "the deathless I"—is not socially determined but personally discovered. Defined by inward potential rather than exterior conditions, this unique identity is to be fulfilled primarily in one's vocation. The final exhortation is reminiscent of Thomas Carlyle, but this theme was also developed by Wordsworth, Keats, John Stuart Mill, and others, as a common legacy of Romantic and Victorian literature. The thwarting of creative potential leaves the individual devoid of an authentic self, in the condition that Coleridge called "Life-in-Death": a circumscribed egotism that Lampman, like Coleridge, expresses in spectral imagery (lines 6–7). This diminished and desiccated self is depicted by Lampman in "Among the Timothy" and

"The Poet's Song" much as it had been described in *The Prelude,
Sartor Resartus,* and Mill's *Autobiography.* Lampman presents an essentially secular concept of salvation as self-realization in this life
rather than eternal bliss in an afterlife. He equivocates on this point
in the sestet, perhaps with an eye on the orthodox sensibilities of
his public. But the opening line of "Salvation" firmly establishes
"Nature" as the ground of the human spirit. Lampman's key terms
whenever he deals with the theme of self-cultivation are "nature"
and "soul"; as in Wordsworth's poetry, references to God are usually
of peripheral significance.

Lampman's concern for the free development of aptitudes no doubt
had a personal bearing. Several of his essays suggest that the artist's
is the most vital of all gifts, and his letters show that he felt that
his own talent was constrained by his obligations to his family and
his work in the civil service. His most scathing remarks are reserved
for the agents of industrial capitalism, which he considered viru-
lently destructive of humane values. Where Blake and Shelley had
leveled their invective at priests and kings, Lampman's targets are
"The Modern Politician" (1890), and another contemporary type in
"To a Millionaire" (1891).

In his thinking about social injustice, Lampman recognized the
inertia of outworn traditions and the role of vested interests devoted
to maintaining privilege, but he stressed the general myopia of
human beings. While he condemned the millionaire and "The
Usurer" (c. 1884) as batteners on misery, he acknowledged that
"the commonest pursuit among men is the pursuit of wealth . . .
a species of madness or mental blindness which is endemic in no
particular country, but has been a universal pestilence affecting every
age and every climate."[15] His radicalism in politics did not extend
to his moral ideas, which remained conservative. If he takes a sec-
ularized view of salvation, his view of evil conjures up a venerable
Christian tradition:

> Blind multitudes that jar confusedly
>   At strife, earth's children, will ye never rest
>   From toils made hateful here, and dawns distressed
> With ravelling self-engendered misery?
> And will ye never know, till sleep shall see
>   Your graves, how dreadful and how dark indeed
>   Are pride, self-will, and blind-voiced anger, greed,

> And malice with its subtle cruelty?
> How beautiful is gentleness. . . .
>   ("Gentleness" [1888?], *PAL,* 108)

Here Lampman approaches a restatement of the seven deadly sins. The crucial terms are two that he repeats for emphasis, and that reflect conflicting tendencies in his understanding of human conduct. "Blindness" is a central metaphor in visionary literature, which affirms the hope that if only people's perceptions can be cleansed, a renovated world will follow. But the execration of "self" belongs to a world-view that regards humanity as innately flawed. Lampman's vision of evil characteristically shifts between a Romantic indictment of circumstances and institutions, and a Christian indictment of human nature. This uncertainty underlies the major deficiency in his political poems: a lack of conviction about remedies. He vigorously attacked injustice and he envisaged a better day, but he was doubtful how to proceed. His urging of "gentleness" upon the blind multitudes is weak, as he probably knew.

Lampman never reconciled his commitment to nature as a moral criterion with his mistrust of "natural" impulses within the psyche. Occasionally he accepts instinct and emotion as essential to human achievement: the "hunger" described in "Winter-Store," "Alcyone," and "The Minstrel" is a force that shatters false convention and fuels creativity. But elsewhere he considers such hunger pernicious, and comes close to the Stoic view that passion is a morbid condition of the soul. For this reason, even while granting that Byron and Rossetti offer insights into the darker areas of the psyche, Lampman rejected their work as "of no real value" and "painful and disagreeable."[16] He wavered painfully between a celebration and a renunciation of desire, and he tended to generalize from his moods. In "Happiness," he discusses with considerable subtlety the conflict of selfishness and conscience in the human personality. But when he turns to the problem of the individual's relation to society, his argument becomes tenuous: "To those natures whose aptitudes and impulses are exceptionally quick and strong, one of the greatest dangers to happiness is the refusal to accept genially the limitations which society has set to the undue expansion of the individual."[17] Our uncertainty about what constitutes "undue expansion" is not relieved when Lampman goes on to counsel acceptance of "the narrow limits of practical life" as the way to "the humanest and most natural liberty." This version of natural liberty makes curious reading beside some of his more vehement denunciations of social inequities.

Lampman's work fluctuates between an activist critique of the social order and a disposition toward contemplative values, including contempt for the world—hence his affinities with Platonism and Christian asceticism. His sympathies with the English Romantics were at odds with his acceptance of a dualistic notion of human experience that the Romantics had been at pains to resolve. He tended to think of flesh and spirit as adversaries rather than complements, and he overrated the power of abstract idealism to dominate the deep forces of instinct and passion. He never really came to grips with the problem of action in an imperfect world, having recourse to a theory that this world is after all unreal, and he was capable of declaring his indifference to social conflict: "I let the wrangling world go by, / And like an idle breath / Its echoes and its phantoms fly . . ." ("Amor Vitae" [1891], *PAL,* 251). If he had lived longer, Lampman might have sorted out the contradictions that rendered his poetic vision unstable. As it was, his work remained a rich disorder of ideas seized upon only to be dropped when his mood changed or his conviction faltered. What is conspicuously absent from his visionary politics is any firm interpretation of the movement of history. Sometimes he indulged his taste for primitivism ("Favorites of Pan"), sometimes his equally strong inclination for the idea of moral evolution ("The Clearer Self"). He also expressed skepticism about *any* change in the human situation ("Xenophanes"), endorsed a revolutionary struggle ("Liberty"), and surmised a catastrophic apocalypse ("War").

Cities of Dream and Nightmare

The most fascinating of Lampman's political visions are focused on the image of the city, and here again there are contradictions. These cities are variously located in present, past, and future; they include historical and imaginary places; and they are described in both naturalistic and symbolic terms. Generally, they form two groups: as centers of iniquity and death, and as beloved communities, they approximate the archetypes of Babylon and Jerusalem. The Apocalyptic City is a familiar archetype. What is striking about its appearance in Lampman's work is that while his vision of Babylon remains constant, his idea of a New Jerusalem varies. He wrote one major poem about the infernal city, and it can stand for most of his minor poems on the same theme. But he wrote three major poems about the paradisal community, which has a different character in each.

Industrialization had invested the biblical image of the vile metropolis with new significance for writers of the nineteenth century. For poets like Lampman, the machine age represented an aggravation of the traditional evils of great cities: the apotheosis of the marketplace, the abuse of power, the debasing of pleasure, and the attenuation of life. One of the recurring patterns in his work, as in English Romantic poetry, is the contrast between this malignant urban domain and the healing realm of nature. In both "The Poet's Song" and "The Minstrel," an archetypal bard leaves the city to find a renewed vision among elemental natural forces, and half a dozen other poems refer to a similar movement from city to countryside. For Lampman, landscape offers an environment sympathetic to emotional and aesthetic capacities that are starved or perverted in the city. The infinitely varied complexion of nature fosters nuances of feeling, and its sublime qualities inspire the human spirit to rise above itself. Above all, nature signifies the creative vitality that sustains human freedom against arbitrary rule. By contrast, the city is oppressive, ugly, and ephemeral.

This view of the city was given consummate expression in one of Lampman's finest poems. "The City of the End of Things" (1892) is a prophetic vision that reflects his interpretation of the conditions of his age; one of its canceled titles is "The Issue of Things That Are." It is more intense and compelling than any of his visions of a New Jerusalem, and to that degree suggests the strength of foreboding that lay behind the principled optimism of his essays. The poem presents an infernal apocalypse that is the logical end of urban corruption and mechanization. He had pictured similar demoniac civilizations in earlier poems: the city "made a tomb" in "The Weaver" (1883), "the great city Roma" in "The Three Pilgrims" (1885), and the agitated contemporary metropolis in "The City" (1888). A number of critics have noted sources for "The City of the End of Things" in Edgar Allan Poe's "The City in the Sea" (1831) and James Thomson's *The City of Dreadful Night* (1880); perhaps Byron's "Darkness" (1816) should be added to the list.[18] Indeed, "The Last Man" became something of a minor convention in early Romantic literature, as the theme of an unfinished play by

Thomas Lovell Beddoes written in 1823, poems by Thomas Campbell (1823) and Thomas Hood (1826), and a novel by Mary Shelley (1826). Lampman's poem is nonetheless a powerful achievement in its own right. Its symbolism is oblique, but becomes clearer in the light of other poems by Lampman and in the wider context of apocalyptic literature.

When the poet says that he hears of the City "in dreams," he is suggesting that the imagination that shapes our lives has gone awry. The City is a projection of current impulses: "Its roofs and iron towers have grown / None knoweth how high within the night" (PAL, 179). The tower, mentioned three times in the poem, is its most prominent symbol. As an image of pride mocked by a ghastly clamor, it has overtones of Babel, but it also has another meaning. In certain Romantic poems, towers symbolize the human consciousness, which becomes both a fortress and a prison of its own beliefs. [19] Throughout Lampman's poetry, towers are almost synonymous with cities, and in "A January Sunset" (1884), "Storm" (1886), and "A Night of Storm" (1887) they suggest a beleaguered or self-divided consciousness. This last implication comes close to the meaning of the iron towers in the City of the End of Things, where intellect has divided itself from the senses. A similar treatment of the image occurs in "Emancipation" (c. 1888–89), a poem also reminiscent of Poe, but never included in any of Lampman's published volumes. As its title might be taken to suggest, it graphically illustrates Lampman's tendency to think in terms of a split between body

> Housed in earthen palaces are we
>   Over smouldering fires,
> Wherethrough the fumes creep witheringly,
>   Doubts and hot desires. . . .

and spirit:

> Yet each palace—this we know—
>   Hath one central tower;
> Round about it breathe and blow
>   Winds for every hour;
> And its spire through ether riven
>   Enters heaven. [20]

Ironically, this rather conventional dualism is precisely what Lampman's more famous poem calls into question. The inhabitants of the City of the End of Things have internalized a mechanical model of existence to the point of extirpating the feeling and creativity necessary for self-renewal. As the City deteriorates, the fires that "moulder out and die" reflect the extinction of imaginative energy that has long since doomed its residents. The visionary faculty is eclipsed, and with it the source of song and poetry. Lampman's emphasis on the inhuman character of the place amplifies its horror as a grim transfiguration of our own society. In this City of the damned, behavior follows neither instinct nor intelligence, but conforms to an imposed pattern. It is the antithesis of the ideal affirmed in Lampman's essays, a community of individuals who realize their identities through nurturing inborn talents. Lampman uses the same sort of image here that he does in "Salvation" to convey the idea of aborted individuality: the empty shell, a variation on the hollow tower.

The infernal features of the City are so many inversions of the values that Lampman saw in natural landscape. Its roaring furnaces, its "ceaseless round" of mechanical action, and its "inhuman music" are demonic counterparts of the sun imagery, the seasonal cycles, and the hymn of nature in *Among the Millet* and *Lyrics of Earth*. As it draws toward an end, the poem focuses on the specters who preside over the City's decline:

> But now of that prodigious race,
> Three only in an iron tower,
> Set like carved idols face to face,
> Remain the masters of its power;
> And at the city gate a fourth,
> Gigantic and with dreadful eyes,
> Sits looking toward the lightless north,
> Beyond the reach of memories;
> Fast rooted to the lurid floor,
> A bulk that never moves a jot,
> In his pale body dwells no more,
> Or mind or soul,—an idiot!
>
> (*PAL,* 181)

I take this strange group to mean two things: a divorce of intellect and corporeality, to the corruption of both; and a division of society into masters and slaves, or any elite supported by an ignorant mass. The gigantic figure stares into an Arctic waste that mirrors his emptiness—a parody of the responsive landscape of Lampman's nature poems. The hierophants in the tower will finally perish, victims of their exaltation of science; then darkness will overtake the City: "Alone of its accursèd state, / One thing the hand of Time shall spare, / For the grim Idiot at the gate / Is deathless and eternal there" (*PAL*, 182). This is a demonic caricature of the universe in human form, the integration of all people and worlds in one enormous Being, as an image of the apocalypse. It also recalls, ironically, the angels who stand at the gates of the New Jerusalem in Revelation 21. In Lampman's nightmare, all men are ultimately abased to their lowest common factor: gross, spiritless flesh. The end of all things is the reduction of all variety and distinction.

Lampman wrote three other poems that envisage an ultimate transformation of human society, but "The City of the End of Things" remains his most impressive apocalypse. "The Land of Pallas," "A Vision of Twilight," and "The Frost Elves" all describe places conceived as beautiful and infinitely appealing, but these visions of the New Jerusalem are neither as compelling nor as charged with insight as his prophecy against Babylon. Ironically, in these poems Lampman retreats from some of his perceptions in "The City of the End of Things," and pictures his ideal communities with certain disconcerting similarities to his infernal city.

"The Land of Pallas" (1891–96) should perhaps be termed Utopian rather than apocalyptic, although there are hints that it describes the millennium after a fiery catastrophe. It owes much—perhaps too much—to William Morris's *News from Nowhere* (1890), and is essentially a verse-narrative rather than a symbolic configuration.[21] It opens with the narrator inexplicably arrived in the Land of Pallas, from which he returns to "a land of baser men," our own imperfect world, at the end. This is the framework of *News from Nowhere,* and indeed the landscape at the outset of Lampman's poem recalls the tranquil Thames setting of Morris's initial chapters. The river is the controlling image of the poem and also, I think, related to its metrical form. The regular, undulating hexameters contribute to the atmosphere of leisure and peacefulness, though at times they verge on the soporific.

Physically, the Land of Pallas turns out to be a mixture of romance landscape and medieval topography. Its cities are "set far off on hills down vista'd valleys" (*PAL,* 202), and it is only when he returns to the present that the narrator actually enters a metropolis. Similarly, in a dozen shorter lyrics Lampman views cities from a distance as harmonized with landscape, transfigured by light into visions of beauty. It is unnecessary, I think, to consider such treatments of the city "a pretty pictorial accessory" or even "a deliberate limitation of subject matter."[22] They are rather extensions, on a small scale, of the tradition that begins with St. John's vision of the holy city in Revelation 21, and continues through Spenser, Bunyan, and others. Lampman never confuses his glimpses of a distant, transfigured city with "reality," which frequently interrupts his visions. They are acts of faith by which he continues to affirm the possibility of a New Jerusalem.

In "The Land of Pallas" Lampman envisages a civilization organized on communist principles, in which there is an equal distribution of labor and produce. He emphasizes its classless structure as "a land of equal gifts and deeds" (*PAL,* 201); evidently its people have not only equal rights but similar degrees of talent as well. It is an almost exclusively agricultural society, having abolished industrial machinery—"engines of forgotten greed" (*PAL,* 206)—as well as all currency and legal institutions, including marriage. In such a community, Lampman suggests, neither contracts nor law enforcement are necessary, "for no man dreamed of hurt, dishonour, or miscarriage, / Where every thought was truth, and every heart was pure" (*PAL,* 205). In this ideal society dreams are apparently as superfluous or regressive as poets in Plato's Republic. In fact there is provision for any such potential troublemakers in the form of a museum that preserves specimens of the machinery, legal codes, and ceremonial "gauds" that caused so much distress in the past.[23] A look at these relics is apparently enough to quell any thoughts of change. The society is sustained through a general altruism inculcated by training and the habits of generations, including evening festivals and other mild rituals:

> Beside smooth streams, where alleys and green gardens meeting
> Ran downward to the flood with marble steps, a throng
> Came forth of all the folk, at even, gaily greeting,
> With echo of sweet converse, jest, and stately song.
>
> (*PAL,* 204)

This "flood" is one of many that flow through the country, waters "so vast and old, men wist not whence they sprang" (PAL, 202)— a line that indicates a primitive consciousness, timeless, undisturbed by scientific curiosity. In fact the people are several times called "children." The river is glimpsed in the opening stanza as a simile for the placid character of life in the Land of Pallas, and here it has the aura of a magical source at the heart of the country.

Thus far, Lampman's Utopia is at least plausible in its consistency, though it does have certain peculiar features. The inhabitants are pictured as an oddly passive breed of romance heroines and heroes: "tall fair women" (PAL, 203) and men "like kings for majesty" (PAL, 205). There are hints of chivalry in their relationship, the reward of "lofty beauty and blithe speech" (PAL, 203) when the men are joined by the women after working in the fields. Lampman strives to invest this peaceful agrarian system with heroic dignity, but in the Utopian context his terms seem a little strained. It is hard to imagine "lofty and impassioned" deeds in a land where "golden calm" (PAL, 202) prevails.

Such paradoxes seem negligible, however, when the narrator comes upon an elevation like the acropolis, from which multitudes come and go. A passerby, who is none other than "a dreamer," informs him that the shining edifice on the mountain is dedicated to "the priestless worship of the all-wise mother," Pallas:

> "There dwell the lords of knowledge and of thought increasing,
>   And they whom insight and the gleams of song uplift;
> And thence as by a hundred conduits flows unceasing
>   The spring of power and beauty, an eternal gift."
>   (PAL, 208)

This is the culmination of the narrator's vision and of the river motif, which is now identified with the wisdom of philosophers and artists. It also echoes the apocalypse described in the Book of Daniel: "many shall run to and fro, and knowledge shall be increased" (12:4)—a vision that comes to the prophet as he stands "by the side of the great river" (10:4). Remarkably, dreams, poets, and science suddenly materialize as the honored nucleus of a society that has been described as suspicious of innovative thinking. Neither here nor elsewhere has Lampman resolved the old paradox that knowledge is both a blessing and a curse. More significantly, the ostensibly egalitarian society of his Utopia sorts itself out after all, into an elite who dwell symbolically above the quiescent mass—a startling parallel to the hierophants in the tower of "The City of the End of Things." Morris's pleasant horizontal anarchy has been crossed with Plato's hierarchy in a mixture that behaves like water and oil.

The conclusion of the poem brings into still clearer focus the central problem of Lampman's Utopian vision. The narrator returns to our familiar world of injustice and pain, where he becomes a political evangelist, preaching reform. He is rebuked by the ruling class and misunderstood by the oppressed, who smile bitterly "out of hollow orbs" (*PAL,* 209), suffering the deficiency of vision that Lampman commonly ascribes to humanity. Nevertheless, the narrator perseveres: "For well I knew that on and upward without cease / The spirit works for ever, and by Faith and Presage / That somehow yet the end of human life is Peace" (*PAL,* 210). The appeal for Lampman (and for us) of the very process of spiritual growth undermines his picture of a static, perfected social order with child-adults and a doctrinal disapproval of change. Had he hit upon some such idea as Blake's notion of a progressive strife of contraries and continuing "Wars of Love" in the New Jerusalem, he might have resolved his contradictions.[24] As it is, "The Land of Pallas" remains an unstable concoction of Hellenic imagery, Utopian socialism, biblical apocalypse, and romance.

Furthermore, the final line of the poem is loaded with unintentional irony: *in pace requiescat.* The end of life brings peace in a sense very different from what Lampman means in his Utopian prophecy, but this other sense of the word also appealed to him. To say that he was possessed by a death-wish would be glib, but at times he did see death as an attractive alternative to his abating faith in nature, his anxieties about the social order, and the strain of his relations with his wife and Katherine Waddell. Tired with all these, at certain moments he fancied an ultimate rest. He expressed these feelings in two moving sonnets, "Death" (1891) and "In Beechwood Cemetery" (1894), and they also pervade his two final visions of an apocalyptic city.

In "A Vision of Twilight" (1895), at one stage titled "City of the Spirit," Lampman presents a celestial counterpart to the temporal visions of "The City of the End of Things" and "The Land of Pallas." The first stanza recalls the opening lines of the other poems, but

now the poet's dream evokes an absolutely discarnate realm. The
pounding cataracts of the doomed city and the placid currents of
Utopia are replaced by a river without content or vicissitude, an
ideal river, of pure form. Lampman's twilight city is fascinating in
its relation to the other provinces of his dreams. Ironically, the
language employed to sketch this heaven is also that of the spectral
world of life-in-death that he abhors in his nature lyrics. Here he
embraces shadows rather than exorcising them in a vision of minute
particulars. "In its courts and hallowed places / Dreams of distant
worlds arise . . ." (*PAL*, 195): an infinite regression, dreams within
a dream. Like Poe, whose cadences haunt this poem, Lampman feels
the natural world recede—but he welcomes its eclipse. One stubborn
piece of landscape remains: a garden, Lampman's symbol for the
cultivated imagination. This compounds the irony when he writes
that at dusk "my city rounds and rises, / Like a vapour formed afar"
(*PAL*, 198). His edifice appears in the manner of one of the memorable precincts of Milton's vision: not the Garden of Eden, not
Heaven, but Pandemonium.

Notwithstanding these ironies, Lampman's twilight city represents a personal conception of heaven that borrows heavily from
Christian tradition while avoiding explicitly Christian reference. Its
most striking departure from Christian iconography is in the absence
of God and the angels. Lampman's heaven is an egalitarian community rather than a spiritual hierarchy. Its inhabitants are the
immortal souls of men and women after their bodily demise; curiously, they remain identifiable as sexes, despite their disembodied
state. Purged of mortal pride and "quick with love and pity" (*PAL*,
196), they are also omniscient. Freed from the uncertainties of
empirical knowledge and human memory, they comfort the rapt
poet with parables:

> In a tongue that once was spoken,
>   Ere the world was cooled by Time
> When the spirit flowed unbroken
>   Through the flesh, and the Sublime
> Made the eyes of men far-seeing,
>   And their souls as pure as rain,
> They declare the ends of being,
>   And the sacred need of pain.
>   (*PAL*, 197)

This is Lampman's weak version of a theodicy. Unable to affirm an orthodox faith, he rehearses Christian ideas without transforming or illuminating them. His immortals appeal to the argument from design in declaring the cosmos purposive (*PAL,* 198), but their justification of suffering goes without any amplification, except for the hint at a myth of the Fall, which jostles with the geological image in the stanza quoted above. Significantly, Lampman sees the prelapsarian condition as a harmony of flesh and spirit, now permanently lost; hence his eagerness to dispense with flesh altogether in this ethereal city. In the final stanza, however, all conviction fails him and he ends in indecision, questioning the truth of his vision.

Although "The Frost Elves" was composed earlier, in 1893, it is a more extreme expression of motives implicit in "A Vision of Twilight." It is, however, free of clumsy appropriations of Christian tradition; instead, Lampman adapts the supernatural frame of the poem from folklore. On a winter's night the speaker dreams a visitation. Two eyes peer at him through his frosted window, then disappear, leaving an elfin poem traced upon the pane; his translation of this mysterious script follows: "A city of amber stands withdrawn / On the opaline edge of the west" (*ALS,* 6). Though located in the land of the frost elves, it is not their city. The elves are mysterious nature-spirits, marvelously quick; the inhabitants of the city are the motionless spirits of once impassioned mortals, now eternally mute on its battlements: "Peasants and emperors, old and young, / They fronted the low sunrise, / They sat with no sound; and the hoar frost hung / In the width of their passionless eyes" (*ALS,* 6). These frozen souls are the complement of the hulking body stationed "deathless and eternal" at the gate of the City of the End of Things. Here, too, all variety and change are obliterated, but now such repose seems lovely. Both "The Frost Elves" and "A Vision of Twilight" describe realms whose inhabitants are free of human desire and struggle; however, while Lampman's twilight city represents a heaven where life continues on the supernatural plane, with wisdom, purpose, and the conversation of spirits, his amber city is patently a city of death, frozen, silent, and beautiful—a remarkably pure expression of a death-wish, virtually unmitigated by the consolations of the traditional religious imagination.

In "The City of the End of Things" Lampman expressed his intuition that a philosophy which divides spirit against flesh has destructive implications for individuals and societies alike. A similar insight is one motive of his landscape poetry, which resumes Wordsworth's attempt to reconcile the mind of man with nature. However, Lampman refused to make this intuition the basis of a comprehensive vision. In the face of persistent strife within himself and in the world abroad, he rejected a principle of integration and reaffirmed a divisive myth of repression and renunciation. As a result, his visionary communities in "The Land of Pallas," "A Vision of Twilight," and "The Frost Elves" are all in some measure cities of the end of things. As Dick Harrison says, apropos of these and other poems: "what Lampman gives us is less a silence of contemplation or peace than a fascinated hovering on the edge of the ultimate silence of death."[25] Of all Lampman's poems, "The Frost Elves" suggests the most extreme ironies. Toward the end of "Winter-Store" the poet had shuddered at the menacing brilliance of the Aurora, and in "The City of the End of Things" he left his gigantic idiot staring with ghastly eyes toward a "lightless north." Perhaps these moments of revulsion are so intense because Lampman was also attracted toward an Arctic annihilation of consciousness. His city in the land of the frost elves, with its icy emerald battlements and crystal walls, is an extraordinary variation on the bejeweled holy city in the Apocalypse of St. John: a devoutly wished universe of death rather than a resurrection to eternal life.

These mutations of the apocalyptic city show how much Lampman's vision shifted with his moods. He was passionately committed to social change, but in extremis he identified redemption with paralyzed oblivion. While at times he shows considerable acuteness about politics, as often his vision seems based on wishful thinking rather than on the drama of human relations. Lampman both yearned for and recoiled from human contact, an ambivalence that he expressed as early as 1884, in "What Do Poets Want With Gold?" This little lyric is divided into two parts that neatly reflect Lampman's divided impulses. The first section attacks the love of money, and suggests that the poet's vocation is to bring "human hearts" into relation. Then the theme changes abruptly: "What do poets want with love? / Flowers that shiver out of hand, / And the fervid fruits that prove / Only bitter broken sand?" (PAL, 51). The first part of the poem insists on the poet's social significance and on the value of experience; the second pictures the poet as a solitary dreamer who does well to avoid the contamination of experience. However conventional these lines may sound, they are sharply relevant to any general interpretation of Lampman's work. Between his ideas and his realities, there was shadow. Romantic love became the conception through which he tried to unify his ideas about human destiny. It was his misfortune that his erotic idealism would suffer an even more severe bruising than his veneration of nature.

Chapter Six
Romantic Love

Early Love Poems

Lampman's love poems can be best appreciated in two contexts: the great tradition of English amatory verse, and the circumstances of his personal relationships. The structural elements were art and life, and the connection between them was, in Lampman's case, ineluctably Romantic. Twentieth-century criticism has taught us to be suspicious of easy connections between poet and persona; still, certain lyrics compel our sense of their identity. Biographical information remains invaluable to the interpretation of many poems, provided that we maintain due respect for their integrity and complexity. I do not wish to explain Lampman's work in terms of his life, but to recognize the biographical elements and to explore their relation to the conventional features. Such an inquiry is necessary to our understanding of Lampman's achievement, for romantic love became his master theme after 1890 and crucially affected his career as a poet during that last, truncated decade.

Although much of Lampman's love poetry is indebted to Elizabethan models, it remains essentially Romantic in several ways. Renaissance poets generally maintained a distinction (if not an antithesis) between divine love and sexual love. The English Romantics, especially Shelley and Keats, had less confidence in divine love and were inclined to exalt the most intense of human relations in its place. Their pursuit of an illumination through erotic experience parallels their approach to nature. In Lampman's work, the "dreams" that signify imaginative fruition in his nature poems correspond to, and sometimes merge with, the dream of erotic fulfillment in his love poetry. And like his Romantic precursors, Lampman reveals a profound uneasiness about the destructive implications of sexual enchantment. There is an unmistakable convergence of Eros and Thanatos in some of the love poems, as well as in those nature lyrics that present the seasonal cycle as an erotic myth involving male and female figures. The Romantic poet tends to see his beloved much as he sees his landscapes, as a reflection of all that is best within himself: a sublime illusion, doomed to founder on the shores of experience. This collision of desire with knowledge yields romantic irony, which cherishes illusions even as it illumines their inadequacy. Such a subversion of the ideal by the real also implies the biographical factor in Romantic love poetry: for most Romantics, a conception of love both shapes and is shaped by their lives.

The love poetry that Lampman wrote during his involvement with Katherine Waddell is continuous with his love poetry of the 1880s, written during his courtship and early marriage. Whatever the details of his life with Maud and his affair with Katherine, in both cases Lampman idealized his partner and was disappointed, albeit for different reasons. It was his abiding conviction that for each of us is born a "kindred spirit" with whom to consummate our destinies. The phrase actually occurs in a lyric written for Katherine in 1897, when he had bleakly accepted that he would not fulfill his love for the woman he considered his soul mate ("Kindred Spirits," *LK,* 50). This notion of soul mates is dangerous; it assumes that successful marriages are ordained by fate rather than sustained through effort, and may have contributed to Lampman's dissatisfaction with Maud. The best evidence that this was the case emerged years later, when E. K. Brown collaborated with Duncan Campbell Scott in editing *At the Long Sault* (1943). According to Brown's notes on a conversation with Scott about Katherine Waddell, "Lampman found his wife unsympathetic to poetry—although she was very devoted to his study and practice of it—and thought that in this girl he would find a spiritual mate. The idea of spiritual affinities was very important to Lampman: he often spoke of it in general terms to Scott. His wife was not such an affinity."[1] For Lampman, both the ecstasy of requited love and the suffering of unhappy love turned on the chance of finding a kindred spirit. While at times he could be critical of the idea, it pervades his love poetry from beginning to end.

Among Lampman's earliest love poems are the sonnets written for Maud during their courtship in 1884–85, and arranged by Scott as "The Growth of Love" in *At the Long Sault*. In a letter to Brown, Scott opined that "these Sonnets have their root in Rosetti {*sic*}; the form of address My Lady &c reminiscent of the House of Life and sometimes the phrases. . . ."[2] There is, however, much more of the Elizabethan sonneteers, especially Spenser, than there is of Rossetti in "The Growth of Love." Rossetti's sonnets in "The House of Life" have far more analytical force, as well as a more explicit sexual content, and were mostly written in the poet's maturity, against a sophisticated, continental background. Lampman's sonnets were written by a young man of limited experience and provincial upbringing, and are far more conventional. They are apprentice-work, but if their substance is derivative, their technical competence foreshadows Lampman's excellence in the form.

Apart from a recurring emphasis on his Lady's childlike character, "The Growth of Love" reflects few of the circumstances of Lampman's relation to Maud. The sonnets remain rigorously Spenserian in conceit and language. They include a rhetorical exercise in antithesis (I), catalogs of the Lady's merits (II, VI.I), and an allegory of the lover's soul (V). The speaker rehearses the standard Petrarchan situation ("When I would woo my love, she turns aside"), with the typical oxymorons ("sweet pain"), and the usual symptoms. As it happened, Spenser's "Amoretti," which records the eventual resolution of the poet's hopes and fears in marriage, was just the model for Lampman. Sonnet VIII (1884), for example, might be taken to register a turning point in his courtship of Maud.

There are two things especially worth noting in this poem and in its companions. One is the idea that sexual love has an essentially religious meaning, a convention that Lampman adopted quite seriously. The other is the dream motif, which persists in his love poetry, as it does in his work as a whole. In Sonnets IX and XI Lampman considers the possibility that the dream of bliss that he shares with his Lady will dissolve with time. It is a typically Spenserian concern with mutability, but from our vantage point these poems are also rather poignant in view of the turn Lampman's marriage later took.

The main features of Lampman's love poetry are all present in the love poems included in *Among the Millet* (1888). They reflect precisely that tension between desire and experience so typical of Romantic literature, and the first of them dramatizes this tension in a narrative vignette. The speaker of "Between the Rapids" (1886) is a voyageur whose travels have returned him after five years to the stretch of a river that runs by the farm where his beloved lived. He envisages love as the foundation of a pastoral, domestic existence, a "dream" that he is unable to realize as he is swept onward by life's currents: "Aye thus it is! Heaven gleams and then is gone: /

Once, twice, it smiles, and still we wander on" (*PAL*, 38). If it did not illustrate certain elements that become crucial in Lampman's love poetry, we would probably sooner ignore this tissue of Arnoldian cadences and forced nostalgia.[3] It anticipates, however, the counterpoise of journeying against domestic love in two much better poems, "An Athenian Reverie" and "The Story of an Affinity." Furthermore, the voyageur's idealized picture of his lost love, Virginie, is most significant: "And is she changed, or is her heart still clear / As wind or morning, light as river foam? / Or have life's changes borne her far from here, / And far from rest, and far from help and home?" (*PAL*, 37). The subtext here is the displacement of lover by landscape. The speaker identifies his beloved with his wandering way of life, and in that measure she is a projection of himself, a creature of his imagination more than a woman known of old. Little wonder, then, that he submits to currents which sweep away from a place that might confront him with a challenge not only to his idealized image of her, but to his own unsated wanderlust as well.

"The Monk" and "An Athenian Reverie," two narratives on a larger scale, elaborate these tensions: the former represents sheer desire, while the latter assumes the more critical standpoint of experience. "The Monk" (1886), a tale in forty-seven stanzas of ottava rima, depicts a triumph of love. Done in the manner of Keats's "The Eve of St. Agnes" with heavy-handed Gothic touches, it has had no praise from Lampman's critics, and, like any Gothic tale, seems preposterous until we look for its symbolic meaning. In a sense, the theme of "The Monk" *is* "dream": the word, which occurs a dozen times, is subjected—in the distress of the forlorn lover, Nino, and in the story of the mysterious monk who visits him—to criticism and scorn, only to be redeemed toward the end. As in "The Eve of St. Agnes," the beloved materializes in the lover's chamber as though summoned by sheer desire:

> She dashes from her brow the pented hood;
>   The dusky robe falls rustling to her feet;
> And there she stands, as aye in dreams she stood.
>   Ah, Nino, see! Sure man did never meet
> So warm a flower from such a sombre bud,
>   So trembling fair, so wan, so pallid sweet.

> Aye, Nino, down like saint upon thy knee,
> And soothe her hands with kisses warm and free.
>
> (*PAL,* 86)

The sinister robes of an obsolete religion are sloughed off to reveal the lovely incarnation of a new and living faith, the creed of romantic love. Indeed, the emphasis throughout is on fidelity: each lover doubts the other but in the end their mutual faith triumphs. The Gothic form is skewed here in that the immediate focus never leaves the lovers; the villains of the piece are known only by report. Moreover, the male protagonist is strictly passive and the female represented as his savior. Lampman's poem, then, is Gothic only superficially, and sentimental in its essence. Bookish Nino, whom thought neither avails nor comforts, is redeemed by a conspicuously active heroine. It is the fantasy of a passive male temperament with inordinate expectations of women.

These attitudes are considered more dispassionately in "An Athenian Reverie" (c. 1885–88). This long narrative monologue portrays in its speaker Lampman's alter ego, the self-conscious artist who considers romantic love both illusory and a hindrance to his creative freedom. One of the finest poems in *Among the Millet,* it is among the few works in which Lampman attempted a synthesis of impulses, as distinct from the hazardous balance of poems such as "Between the Rapids." The dramatic situation in the latter typifies Lampman's tendency to waver between extremes. The long, leisurely reverie of the Athenian, richly appreciative of past and present, is a very different achievement. In this poem Lampman approaches Keats's ideal in "Hyperion": "to envisage circumstance, all calm, / That is the top of sovereignty" (II. 204–5). What makes "An Athenian Reverie" a minor success rather than a grand failure like "Hyperion" is its ultimate evasion of the issues of passion, pain, and loss with which Keats grappled in his splendid but abortive epic. Indeed, Lampman underscores the Athenian's sense that for all his breadth of experience and aesthetic sensitivity, he has not probed life to its depth; and it is this turning of his critical awareness upon himself that sustains the poem's integrity.

Like "The Monk," "An Athenian Reverie" reflects upon various meanings of the word "dream." In the second poem, however, the dream of erotic love is revealed as spurious, attractive only by contrast with the disturbing dreams of sleep and the "dull dream" of wealth and power that constrains the waking hours of most men. The Athenian is Lampman's spokesman for a superior sort of dream: the intense yet detached consciousness that expresses itself in reverie or art. This monologue of the mid-1880s dramatizes the belief implicit everywhere in Lampman's early landscape poetry: the apocalyptic principle that consciousness and art can become one, transforming the quality of human life:

> For see how rich a thing
> Life is to him who sees, to whom each hour
> Brings some fresh wonder to be brooded on,
> Adds some new group or studied history
> To that wrought sculpture, that our watchful dreams
> Cast up upon the broad expanse of time,
> As in a never-finished frieze, not less
> The little things that most men pass unmarked
> Than those that shake mankind.
>
> (*PAL*, 98)

The Athenian's insistence on preserving his bachelorhood and indulging his wanderlust, as opposed to seeking fulfillment in a woman's love, is essentially a manifesto for artistic liberty. This poem, together with "What Do Poets Want with Gold?" (1884) and "The Organist" (1884), expresses an apprehension that sexual love may in some way impair poetic creativity. The poems are moments of skepticism unequal to that apotheosis of romantic love that preoccupied Lampman's imagination in the early 1890s.

The Athenian, who as groomsman is charged with standing watch outside the chamber of the newlyweds Lysippe and Theron, is both sympathetic toward and profoundly critical of romantic love. In one of the poem's finest passages, he celebrates the ecstasy of the nuptial bed; his detached musing leads him, however, to the thought that even sexual bliss is subject to "sad recession," and to a more perplexed view of passion:

> Ai! Ai! 'tis a strange madness
> To give up thought, ambition, liberty,
> And all the rooted custom of our days,
> Even life itself for one all pampering dream,
> That withers like those garlands at the door;
> And yet I have seen many excellent men
> Besotted thus, and some that bore till death,

> In the crook'd vision and embittered tongue,
> The effect of this strange poison, like a scar,
> An ineradicable hurt;
>
> (*PAL*, 96)

This is Lampman's strongest judgment against the dream that informs much of his own work. The Athenian renounces Aphrodite, who reigns in the marriage chamber, and honors "Dian," whose image is painted on a nearby wall: as the adversary of romantic love she embodies the muse that demands fidelity and rewards him with harmonious vision. Yet there is the persistent suggestion that such harmony is achieved by avoiding the deepest "riddles" of life, which can be penetrated only through immersion in the destructive element. There is also the suggestion that in dismissing erotic love as illusion, the Athenian has darkened his mind. In rejecting Aphrodite he displaces his affection: much of the poem extols his friendship with Euktemon, another man who has apparently forsworn women; even their first meeting is recalled, in terms familiar in Lampman's love poetry, as the sudden recognition of kindred spirits. The narrative makes it clear that desire remains a disturbing power in their world and that like their creator, neither has been able to eradicate the dream of an ideal erotic fulfillment.

The English Romantics understood more clearly than Lampman the destructive aspects of a relation that requires in the beloved a reflection of one's soul. They represented this side of romantic love in the theme of incest and in variations upon the myth of Narcissus— two motifs largely absent from Lampman's poetry. In "The Islet and the Palm" (1895) he refers in all innocence to a "gentle sister spirit" and feels no threat in the distant sea to his islanded soul— no hint of the solipsism that whelms Byron's Manfred and the Poet in Shelley's "Alastor." Lampman, indeed, dreamed of sexual love as a release from consciousness, an oblivion in which all anxiety might be drowned. Even the Athenian, most critical of his spokesmen, imagines in a passage of remarkable beauty the rapture of his friends in their marriage chamber:

> Within the silent thalamos the queen,
> The sea-sprung radiant Cytherean reigns,
> And with her smiling lips and fathomless eyes
> Regards the lovers, knowing that this hour

Is theirs once only. Earth and thought and time
Lie far beyond them, a great gulf of joy,
Absorbing fear, regret and every grief,
A warm eternity: or now perchance
Night and the very weight of happiness,
Unsought, have turned upon their tremulous eyes
The mindless stream of sleep; nor do they care
If dawn should never come.

(PAL, 94)

Sleep and Eros are twin themes in Lampman's love poetry, whether in such conventional exercises as "Before Sleep" (1885), or in a number of later poems that seem more personal in their intense enactment of an awakening from sweet dreams to forlorn anguish.[4] A further dimension of the theme emerges in "In Absence" (1890):

My love is far away and I am grown
A very child, oppressed with formless glooms, . . .

(PAL, 265)

and again in "Euphrone" (1894):

O soft-cheeked mother, O beloved night,
Dispeller of black thoughts and mortal dreads,
Drowner of sorrows. . . .

(PAL, 261)

There is the suggestion of infantile regression in the speaker's invocation of night as a mother, as well as in his anxious dependence on his beloved. Both represent an eclipse of consciousness, a resolution of all fear and pain in the warm, dark comfort of the womb.

Of course the remaining analogy, one which poets have always marked, is with death. In Lampman's poetry the relation between sleep, love, and death is associated with the wine cup, at once a female image, an emblem of both delight and degradation, and another symbol of the drowned consciousness. This image appears most strikingly in "The Monk," where the poisoned chalice brought to Nino by the disguised Leonora has a symbolic aura out of all proportion to its narrative function. There is no need whatever in terms of plot or plausibility that the cup really contain poison; that it does is made quite clear. As a symbol, it invites two interpre-

tations. On the one hand, it suggests a parody of the Eucharist—
a lethal draught borne by a figure in ecclesiastical garb. This is
standard Gothic procedure, designed to produce the obligatory fris-
son, but has little to do with the poem's central theme. On the
other hand, there is considerable relevance to the myth of romantic
love in the suggestion of sexuality that the goblet evokes. It is "the
lover's draught, that shall be cure for all" (PAL, 85), and is described
expressively at the critical moment, when Leonora knocks it away
from Nino's lips: "And from his hand the deadly cup hath sped, /
Dashed to the ground, and all its seeded store / Runs out like blood
upon the marble floor" (PAL, 86). This association of a deadly
potion with genital imagery in a poem that honors romantic love
might suggest that like many Romantics in the later nineteenth
century, Lampman was ambivalent about sex and as apt to associate
it with death as with life.

It is exactly this ambivalence that emerges in his use of the goblet
image elsewhere. In "The Growth of Love" III (1884), the poet
envisages his lady as a beautiful queen bearing to her husband "the
golden cup" (ALS, 38). In two rhapsodic nature lyrics, "Spring on
the River" (1883) and "The Sun Cup" (c. 1888–89), the earth is
described as a vessel of the sun's potency. And in "The Story of an
Affinity" (1894), we are given this judgment on the heroine's ca-
lamitous error in rejecting the hero: "She had beat down the true
and perfect love, / And dashed away the sparkling cup of life" (PAL,
466). On the other hand, Lampman is equally apt to suggest in the
image Circe's cup, the degradation of mind and spirit in sensual
surfeit, as he does in "What Do Poets Want with Gold?" (1884),
"The Cup of Life" (1889), and the essay "Happiness" (1895). This
varied use of the symbol signifies two things about Lampman's view
of love. The first, and more demonstrable, is that like most love
poets in the great tradition, he believed in the vital importance of
sexual love as the unifying expression of the carnal and spiritual
elements in human nature. This is the view implicit in many of his
own poems, as well as in his scattered critical remarks on the love
poetry of other writers, where he values intensity while condemning
egotism and the absence of a spiritual element.[5] It seems to me,
however, that his poetry also indicates, perhaps on a less conscious
level, some reaction to the physical realities of sex. Whether Victorian prudery or an idiosyncrasy, it is not an uncommon attitude
in men who idealize women in the extreme.

Stories of Affinity

The scope of Lampman's romantic idealism is plain in two long poems on which he worked between 1891 and 1894, the period during which his love for Katherine Waddell germinated. The first of these is a dramatic poem in blank verse that he took up in the autumn of 1891, having composed it (as he wrote to Thomson) "years ago, when I was only a youngster"; subsequently he referred to it as "my white elephant" and "my Biblical fraud," and he doubted that it would ever be published (*CLT,* 19, 22, 25, 119). "David and Abigail" is as ponderous as Lampman's epithet suggests, but remains important as a study for the much more ambitious narrative he wrote in 1893–94, "The Story of an Affinity." In both, the theme of romantic love is linked to a larger concern about the deficiencies of the social order. In 1892 Lampman wrote two essays defending feminism as the key to a radical improvement in civilization, but contrary to some feminists, he continued to regard romantic love as the best relation between the sexes.[6] No longer sure of the redemptive virtue of nature, and on the threshold of an intense personal attachment, he reaffirmed his hopes for humanity in dreams of an apocalypse by love.

Based on 1 Samuel 25, "David and Abigail" dramatizes the encounter of the two biblical figures as the crucial event in the history of Israel, and by implication, in the history of the world. This is a drastic deviation from the traditional Christian view, which emphasizes the Resurrection as the central event in the human past. Indeed David is portrayed as a type of Christ insofar as he chooses— thanks to Abigail—mercy over vengeance as the basis of a new order. He is gifted with "the prophet's dream, the valour of a king" (*PAL,* 374), the traditional combination of virtues in an ideal leader— wisdom and courage. He is also a microcosm of conflicting impulses, compassion and wrath, and requires Abigail's influence to prevent his killing her odious husband, Nabal. Abigail is portrayed as a living contradiction to the antifeminist slanders with which David greets her, but she is also idealized in what might be regarded as a more subtle form of sexism. As his "Mermaid Inn" essays make clear, Lampman believed that female emancipation would produce not merely greater justice in human relations, but "a type of women of which we can only dream—natural queens among men, to whom they shall look up, as the Goths of old did to their Abruna women, superhumanly beautiful, superhumanly wise" (*MI*, 27 August 1892, 138). This is precisely Abigail's role: she represents not only the charity and vitality that foster human potential, but also truth in the garb of beauty. Her "woman's heart" intuitively understands "the minds of men" (*PAL*, 378), and her destiny, long deferred to duty in a mediocre marriage, is to be a "great woman": that is, an inspiration to the great man. As her cousin Miriam puts it in a speech obviously intended to magnify the reunion of the protagonists:

> The vision of the wise, fair woman, tall
> And glorious, of the potent flute-like speech,
> Who turned his anger from the quest of blood,
> Glows with a light unceasing, uneclipsed,
> Set like a star within the heart of David.
>
> (*PAL*, 405)

It is an image of woman that recurs in Lampman's work, notably in "The Land of Pallas," and it is doubtless the light in which he saw Katherine Waddell. Today it may strike us as a trite and ultimately pernicious form of sentimentality.

"The Story of an Affinity" is more successful in creating a vision of love as the condition of human achievement. Although it has seldom been treated respectfully (if at all) by Lampman's critics, still it is his one impressive attempt at a major narrative poem.[7] Its flaws—passages of melodrama, intervals of flatness, stylistic lapses—are incidental.[8] For the most part its blank verse is supple and unobtrusive, an effective medium for storytelling, close to Words-worth's manner in "The Ruined Cottage" and "Michael," which it echoes several times and resembles in part. But where "Michael" focuses upon a shepherd whose deepest hope is devastated when his son succumbs to the corruption of urban life, "The Story of an Affinity" tells of a farmer's son who exceeds his father's hopes in developing intellectual and moral strength in the city. This trans-formation of Wordsworth's plot no doubt reflects Lampman's New World optimism against the elegiac strain in nineteenth-century English pastoral. The other principal formal influence upon the poem is also a nineteenth-century version of pastoral, the domestic idyll, particularly as developed by Tennyson in "The Gardener's Daughter," "Aylmer's Field," and "Enoch Arden." Like Tennyson's poems, "The Story of an Affinity" is not, for all its modern setting

and homely detail, an essentially naturalistic work. Its meaning is
ultimately mythopoeic, and the myths it evokes are two that have
had special appeal to Canadian writers among both Lampman's
contemporaries and his successors.

The first of these is the myth of Odysseus, as a variation of the
archetypal Romantic quest. The spiritual development of the hero
through a "circuitous journey" is one of the central patterns in the
work of the English Romantics and their inheritors.[9] The Odysseus
myth, which makes sexual love the primary motive of the wanderer's
return, is the characteristic Canadian version, beginning with the
finest nineteenth-century poem written by a Canadian, Isabella Valancy Crawford's "Malcolm's Katie," a work with which Lampman's
narrative deserves close comparison. In "The Story of an Affinity,"
Richard Stahlberg, a youth of heroic potential, is struck with awareness of his self-negligence and a thirst for knowledge when he falls
in love with the daughter of a neighboring farmer. Determined to
develop in himself the spiritual force he sees in her, Richard spends
ten years in the city learning from books and life. The imagery of
sea-wandering that pervades this landbound tale implies his psychological adventuring and inward heroism. He returns just as
Margaret is about to accept another suitor, and eventually she acknowledges Richard as her kindred spirit and destined mate.

The crucial factor in Lampman's treatment of this motif is its
fusion with a second myth: the story of Genesis, especially as told
by Milton in *Paradise Lost*. Like most of the English Romantics,
Lampman undertook in his major narrative to amend the Miltonic
vision of fallen man; like Shelley and Keats, he turns Genesis, and
Milton, inside out by affirming sexual love as a redemptive principle.
Richard's odyssey of worldly experience and self-realization begins
and ends with evocations of the famous closing of *Paradise Lost,* and
these passages, in ironically echoing Milton, suggest homecoming
rather than exile, a recovery rather than a loss of paradise. There
are exact parallels in the resolutions of two important poems by
Lampman's contemporaries, Charles G. D. Roberts's "Orion" and
(again) "Malcolm's Katie." Lampman's momentous discovery of
"Orion" shortly after its publication in 1880 is well known; and it
is quite possible that he also knew Crawford's poem, published in
Toronto in 1884.[10] In any case, all three Canadian poets were par-
ticipants in a characteristic Romantic enterprise that persisted
throughout the century.

In "The Story of an Affinity" Lampman affirms the potential glory of an essentially human dispensation, an ideal order largely unrealized in our familiar world of abused power and exploited ignorance, but achieved by Richard and Margaret on a personal level, through each other. Moreover, they become spiritual pioneers, and as teachers, types of a paradise regained for all men and women. This is a Promethean role; hence, "titanic," used frequently to describe Richard's physical size, is doubly appropriate as an epithet. On a more naturalistic level, "The Story of an Affinity" dramatizes Lampman's concept of salvation as the proper cultivation of innate potential. Insisting on romantic love as the catalyst of Richard's destiny, Lampman firmly subordinates the other influences—nature, religion, politics—that control the lives of individuals, and that shaped his own poetry.

If as late as 1891 Lampman could insist that "the beauty of external nature" is always sufficient inspiration for a poet, the story of "human life" in his most important narrative represents a decided change in his poetic program. One of his main themes in "The Story of an Affinity" is the limit of nature's dominion in human affairs. What he suggests in this long poem is similar to what he had urged in "On the Companionship with Nature" (1892): that while we properly aspire to a higher condition, the quality of our relation to nature remains a measure of our spiritual health. The residents of the "golden land" where Richard and Margaret grow up are generally like the people reproached in his sonnet for their indifference to Nature: "they / That labour without seeing, that employ / Her unloved forces, blindly without joy" (*PAL,* 258). The gradual erosion of Margaret's spirit during Richard's absence is due partly, we are told, to "the neighbouring life—the life of struggling souls— / Bound in its narrow range of earthly needs" (*PAL,* 449). Paradoxically, it is by rising above a merely "natural" life that one achieves a more rewarding relation to natural things. This is the central theme in part one, which describes Richard's youthful agitation in his obscure sense of undeveloped powers within himself. One symptom of his malaise is indifference to the beauty everywhere around him. In his nineteenth year, on the summer's day that will be pivotal in his life, he goes on an errand to the neighboring farm. He is especially sullen, plunged in his chronic mood of baffled impulse, when:

now a sudden frolic wind-rush came,
And smote the wood, and roared upon its tops,
And down across the level like a sea
Ran out in swift pale glimmering waves. The sound
And moving majesty of wind and wood
Broke even the dull clasp of Richard's heart
And touched his spirit with a passionate thrill.

(PAL, 417)

This is the presence of Pan, an epiphany that manifests the creative virtue of nature. But where Lampman had been content in "Favorites of Pan" (1892) and other lyrics of earth to affirm such moments as the ultimate good, this sudden breeze has an extraordinary effect on his youthful hero. In a passage reminiscent of Wordsworth's "Nutting," Richard seizes a young birch tree and rips it "root, stem and branches" from the earth. The inspiration, inadequately focused, issues in destruction; to advert once more to "On the Companionship with Nature," Richard's action is akin to "those whose hands and crude delights obey / The old brute passion to hunt down and slay" *(PAL, 259)*—a perverse expression of sexual energy.

The sexual factor in human creativity is suggested still more clearly when Richard arrives at his neighbor's farm and, wretched with "mindless grief and impotent hunger" *(PAL, 421)*, happens upon Margaret asleep in the orchard. Here she is the counterpart of those elusive female figures, the tutelary spirits of season or place, who emerge in the most sensuous of Lampman's nature poems. Unlike those evanescent maidens, Margaret does not dissolve into the landscape, but abides Richard's question. In what proves to be his genuine epiphany, he is stung by her human beauty, her "spiritual loveliness," to an awareness of his unformed soul. Determined to realize his own powers, Richard asks for her book as a talisman. In Lampman's transformation of Genesis, love engenders the hero's self-awareness and the promise of a paradise. Returning homeward, Richard is more alive to the "gentle influence" of the surrounding countryside *(PAL, 428)*. Natural beauty, it seems, is an insufficient inspiration for people in general—and for poets—though it can restore and sustain moral resolution. Ultimately the natural landscape is a theater for human decisions. The three crises of the poem, first Richard's, then Margaret's *(PAL, 417, 455, 472)*, find them in the orchard, hands on the fence rails, confronting not nature but themselves.

Parts II and III of the narrative show that laws and institutions are also insufficient to amplify the human spirit. In the end, Richard returns to confront his rival, Vantassel, "a lawyer from a busy neighbouring town" (*PAL,* 451). The latter is a man of property, who lacks Richard's insight that love is primary in ordering human life because it makes social constraint needless. For all its mythological reverberation, "The Story of an Affinity" turns on an elementary idea of love, as its title indicates. Richard's sudden recognition of Margaret as his destined mate is a circumstance familiar in Lampman's love poetry, and though her response waits until his return from the city, it comes with the same force of a revelation. Each discovers in the other the enchanting presence so typical in Romantic literature: an idealized projection, or reflection, of the self. The metaphor commonly invoked for this discovery is, of course, "dream": a word that beats like a pulse through the narrative. To mention only the most obvious analogue, we may recall *Endymion,* as well as Keats's reference to Adam's dream of Eve: "he awoke and found it truth" (letter to Benjamin Bailey, 22 November 1817). Indeed at different times both Richard and Margaret have experiences like Nino's in "The Monk": each appears before the other as though created by desire, in a dream (*PAL,* 457, 472). Richard's vision inspires him with heroic purpose, and Margaret's relation to him as an incarnation of virtue is the same as Abigail's to David. "The Story of an Affinity" does secrete some of the sentimentality that spoils Lampman's "Biblical fraud." In general, though, the later poem develops a more balanced view of its hero and heroine. Margaret and Richard are represented as exchanging roles: just as her initial superiority motivates his quest for wisdom, so his eventual reappearance rescues her from a diminished life. The emphasis is on mutuality, as Richard understands: "Henceforth as one / Let us take up the way together, each / Made stronger by the other's loving touch"[11] (*PAL,* 463).

The sexual implications of their relationship are as muted in these lines as in the poem as a whole. Nevertheless, it is clear that the basis of their affinity is physical passion infused with spiritual meaning. Throughout Lampman's poetry the images associated with body and spirit are heat and light. In both "David and Abigail" and "The Story of an Affinity" the protagonists achieve in their union an ideal proportion of the two elements. While both powers are present in both sexes, Lampman generally represents bodily heat as the active principle in his heroes, and spiritual light as the primary force in his heroines. David's "fiery soul" (*PAL,* 389) and Richard's "disordered fire" (*PAL,* 414) require the influence of Abigail and Margaret to release the creative possibilities in their violent natures. Similarly, the women become complete only when their passion is kindled by the men. It is noteworthy that both Abigail and Margaret are associated with the nourishing presence of sunlight, for in this respect Lampman is consistent with the English Romantics who, as one critic has observed, liked to describe love as light from heaven.[12]

"The Story of an Affinity" deals, then, with an issue at the center of Lampman's love poetry: the potential in sexual energy for creation or destruction, in relation to the social order. Among his early narratives, only "An Athenian Reverie"—and with reservations—pictures marriage as both personal fulfillment and valuable ritual. In "The Monk" sexual love is represented as subverting a repressive social order; in a later ballad, "The Emperor's True-Love" (1893), the paramour who "would not be his queen" exults in a power that defies conventions and laws (*ALS,* 11). While "David and Abigail" and "The Story of an Affinity" also celebrate the superiority of love to law, they affirm the socially regenerative potential in passionate love. For Milton, romantic love was a betrayal of one's spiritual integrity, a primary cause of Adam's fall. For Wordsworth (in "Vaudracour and Julia") romantic love represented a betrayal of one's involvement in mankind. Lampman preferred to believe, like Keats's ardent hero, "that it might bless / The world with benefits unknowingly" (*Endymion* I. 826–27).

Toward the end of "The Story of an Affinity," Richard protests that were Margaret to marry Vantassel, they "would find the fate of all unmated things, / The incurable curse of blight and emptiness" (*PAL,* 471). In a shorter narrative poem written the next year, Lampman shows the consequences of such a union. "Ingvi and Alf" (1895) is a verse romance in the Victorian fashion, and an odd rendition of a familiar nineteenth-century plot: the love-rivalry of dark and fair protagonists. The heroine, Bera, marries Alf, one of two brothers who reign together in a Norse kingdom. Whereas Alf is a magisterial figure ("Fond of the tillage of his acres, fond / Of thrift and plenty and well ordered rule" [*PAL,* 348]), his brother Ingvi leads raids on the neighboring coasts. But it is Alf who has the dark features and brooding temperament of a Byronic hero, while the sea-rover Ingvi has a fair countenance and a love of company; that is, Lampman reverses convention in identifying his dark hero with reason and order, and his blond one with instinct and adventure. Bera, though associated with sunlight like Abigail and Margaret, is a rather more erotic figure than her sister-heroines. Indeed, this is the least sexually reticent of Lampman's tales. When Ingvi returns to celebrate his exploits in long nights of feasting, Bera is drawn to the brother with whom she has a genuine affinity. Alf, tormented by jealousy, forbids her to attend the feasts. In the inevitable denouement he awakes one night to an empty bed, and passing into the crowded hall, finds wife and brother in a Freudian tableau, the queen caressing a sword laid across Ingvi's knees:

> On Bera and his brother, ere they knew,
> He came, and plucked the blade out from his cloak
> And made a fearful thrust, and drave it clear
> Through Ingvi's breast, but Ingvi with a cry
> Piercing and wild, reeled up, and heaved his sword
> And smote the head of Alf in twain, and both
> On the grim floorway of the startled hall
> Lay in their mingled blood together—dead.
>
> (PAL, 356)

Understood as psychodrama, "Ingvi and Alf" depicts a lethal division among mind, heart, and libido, and its final line emphasizes the destructive social consequences, in its ghastly parody of brotherhood.

The most intriguing feature of the poem is its sympathy for Alf, who, as an unfit partner for the heroine, corresponds to Nabal and Vantassel, the antagonists in Lampman's other tales. Significantly, Alf is not only an intellectual but "fond too of song-craft" (PAL, 348). On the fatal night when he discovers Bera's disobedience ". . . he woke, disturbed, / Out of a bright and beautiful dream flung back / To hate and horror" (PAL, 355–56). It is an experience described repeatedly in Lampman's poetry, and I think that it is valid to see Alf, in his devastated dream of marital bliss, as a projection of Lampman himself. Sandra Djwa and Bruce Nesbitt have suggested that "David and Abigail" and "The Story of an Affinity" similarly may reflect Lampman's relations with his wife and Katherine Waddell.[13] Though all three narratives deal with triangles of two men and a woman, they can be read as disguised treatments of Lampman's personal situation. Bound by vows to Maud, he felt his true affinity to be with Katherine, and his "Story" is probably to some extent self-justification. Margaret is almost certainly based on Katherine, endowed with the mature grace and "tender" Stoicism that Lampman praised in the latter. Richard, however, is a romantic hero whose confidence and success Lampman could only dream of. The tragic figure, Alf, is probably a closer model of his own mistaken affinity, his own heart's discontent.

Lyrics of Crisis

The love lyrics written in the mid to late-1890s convey this discontent. If Lampman's narratives generally affirm possibilities in which he believed, these shorter poems reflect the realities he suffered. The contradictions that experience raised against his romantic faith were manifold. His belief that love illuminates is crossed by an awareness of the abiding mystery in other human hearts ("Personality" [1893, *PAL*, 185]). The idea that only passion can validate love is crossed by a horrified sense of passion's blindness and deceit ("Love" [1893, *PAL*, 282]). The hope that love can absolve us of our isolation is crossed by a knowledge of our enduring spiritual solitude ("Loneliness" [1894, *ALS*, 26]). And the notion that love can somehow eradicate selfishness is crossed by the dumb persistence of human desire ("Passion" [1896, *PAL*, 279]). For Lampman the result was "Sorrow," the title of one of his frankest sonnets, written in the autumn of 1895:

> At last I fell asleep, and a sweet dream,
> For respite and for peace, was given to me;
> But in the dawn I wakened suddenly,
> And like a fiery swift and stinging stream
> Returned, with fear and horror, the supreme
> Remembrance of my sorrow. All my mind
> Grew hot within me. As one sick and blind,
> Round and still round an old and fruitless theme,
> I toiled, nor saw the golden morning light,
> Nor heard the sparrows singing, but the sweat
> Beaded my brow and made my pillow wet.
> So seared and withered as a plant with blight,

Eaten by passion, stripped of all my pride,
I wished that somehow then I might have died.
                                                     (*PAL,* 281)

This is a virtual microcosm of Lampman's love poetry. Waking from pleasant dreams to a tormented reality is not only a recurring moment in his work, but was also the pattern of his relations with Maud and Katherine. The image of a fiery river is an infernal version of the stream of life, and the blighted plant a parody of the organic metaphor of individual vitality. In this interior conflagration fleshly heat consumes all spiritual light. In the context of Lampman's life and work we can understand that "an old and fruitless theme" has multiple reference: to his passion for a woman, to the theme of so many of his own poems, and to the myth of romantic love that he inherited from the past. That it annuls his delight in natural things is a sign of both its power and its menace. Against his tenacious vision of love, the redeemer, "Sorrow" memorably depicts the ravages of the destroyer, love.

The evidence concerning Lampman's involvement with Katherine is clouded by other problems that contributed to his unhappiness at the time: his frustration in seeking a publisher for his later work, and his anguished suspicion that he was not fully realizing his talent. In the letters to Thomson, certain allusions to his troubles are exasperatingly vague or ambiguous, but they are understandably so if they refer to his romantic imbroglio, given the reticence his sense of honor would demand.[14] In fact, this reticence is attested by Scott, who learned of his friend's relationship with Kate only years after Lampman's death.[15] In 1925 Scott quoted from the letters to Thomson and concluded that they "prove the existence but not the plot of an intense personal drama."[16] Bruce Nesbitt and Margaret Coulby Whitridge have recounted how the "plot" was eventually clarified in the 1940s when E. K. Brown inquired about the hitherto unpublished poems that were to appear as "A Portrait in Six Sonnets" in *At the Long Sault.* The key information came from Lampman's son-in-law, Loftus MacInnes, who identified Katherine Waddell as the lady of the sonnets, and testified that "the attachment gave A. L. profound feeling."[17]

Although some of the conjectures about Lampman and Katherine have been rash, it is clear that from late 1895 to early 1897 their relations underwent a crisis, and that Lampman was forced to relinquish hope of her love. Most of the love poems written in this period were published only after his death, in *At the Long Sault* and *Lampman's Kate*. Many of them are crude and obviously unrevised, and their most prominent characteristic is a heavy dependence on the conventions of Elizabethan love poetry. In "One Woman" (c. 1897, *LK,* 45), for instance, the diction, rhetorical advancement of argument, and Renaissance topos of nature and art recall not only Spenser and Sidney, but the conventions that Lampman had used twelve years earlier in "The Growth of Love." He was quite as eager to see a religious dimension in his love for Kate as he had been in his sonnets for Maud. The key terms throughout "A Portrait" and *Lampman's Kate* are "soul" and "grace," usually referring to poet and lady. The essential motive of these lyrics, however, is the lover's effort to reconcile himself to a sadly frustrated lot: "True love is worth the having, though in vain, / And you worth loving, though the cost be pain!" ("True Passion" [1897?, *LK,* 44]). Perhaps Lampman clung to the belief that he had found his soul mate in Katherine Waddell not despite but because of her reluctance to encourage him. His dissatisfaction in his marriage was due in part to impossible expectations, and had he been free to cultivate relations with Katherine, he might well have suffered disillusionment again. Her unwillingness to return his love probably fed his erotic idealism; hence the Petrarchan convention of reverence and frustration was suited to his circumstances. Far from being an obsolete artifice, Petrarchan love poetry became for Lampman a realistic mode of expression.

While knowledge of Lampman's life sheds some light on these "late love poems," they tell us little that is certain about his relations with Kate. Margaret Coulby Whitridge claims that two poems, "Old Indeed are You" (1896?) and "A Portrait in Six Sonnets" IV (1899), show that Katherine's age was a topic of discussion for them.[18] This is quite possible, though it is also a conventional subject in Elizabethan love poetry, notably in Shakespeare's sonnets. On the other hand, I am convinced that Stoicism, touched upon in "A Portrait" II (1896) and III (1895), was indeed an issue for Lampman and Katherine. Not only is it a common subject elsewhere in his work, but it is also a stance with obvious relevance to their difficult position. Whether or not they were carnal lovers is no doubt the most intriguing human question, if not of the first importance to criticism. Whitridge thinks it probable, on circumstantial evidence.[19] I think not, on the basis of the poems, which stress the limits of their intimacy. In the series of lyrics published

as *Lampman's Kate,* the idea of soul mates acquires bitter irony as
the expressions of thwarted passion recur; similarly, the emphasis
on "friendship" acquires an almost desperate tone by the time Lampman writes "Gold and Dross" in 1897. One is tempted to speculate
about the manuscript of this poem, which has been wholly canceled
in vigorous, sweeping pencil strokes.[20]

While Petrarchism dominated Lampman's love poetry in these
years, he was also writing a handful of lyrics more Romantic in
form and more profound in their treatment of love. The finest of
these is "A Vision of April," dated 28 December 1895, and first
published in *At the Long Sault.* It is a very impressive poem, reminiscent of Blake in its symbolic complexity and ostensible lyric
artlessness. While it has analogues in English Romantic poetry, it
is also the consummate ordering of a distinctive cluster of images
in Lampman's work. Its achievement is in a revealing coordination
of two of his central concerns: the imaginative response to nature,
and the meaning of romantic love. The focal image is an apparition
of April in human form. This feature will recall many pieces in
Among the Millet and *Lyrics of Earth,* in which the poet imagines
seasons or months "as dreamers of old time were wont to feign, /
In living form of flesh" ("June," 1890, *PAL,* 142). But the figure
evoked in "A Vision of April" is more than traditional and em-
blematic; to the poet she means something quite personal, as well:
"April fashioned by a spell / Like a Lady I love well" (*ALS,* 9). Not
a lady, but a Lady; which is to say, not merely Katherine Waddell,
but Lampman's ideal conception of her. Less than two months previously he had written a sonnet praising Katherine: "For when I
think of her I seem to see / April herself among the sunny woods /
With laughing brooks and little clouds that pass; / I dream of
bluebirds and hepaticas" ("A Portrait in Six Sonnets" III, *ALS,* 44).
Virtually the same set of images appears in a sonnet composed in
1890, "Winter-Break" (*PAL,* 252), which describes the poet's dream
of April during a midwinter thaw. But the imagery that in "Winter-
Break" evokes a relaxed spring scene, and that in "A Portrait"
furnishes a pleasant conceit for Katherine, becomes taut and symbolic in "A Vision of April." This later, longer poem is simulta-
neously about nature and nature poetry, romantic love in general,
and Lampman's own relation to Katherine.

The opening stanzas describe a scene that is familiar, yet somehow
different from the landscapes of Lampman's earlier poetry: a meadow

with bare trees that cast "a net of lucid shadow" on the grass, and beyond, a wood with flowers and budding maples. There is an uncanny feeling about this place that is partly accounted for in the poem's first words: "In my dream . . ." (*ALS*, 8). Dreams usually emerge in the course of Lampman's nature lyrics to affirm and complete the reconciliation of mind with nature; here, his dream is the starting point. While most of his nature poems imply some representation of an outward scene together with a symbolic reflection of inward experience, the landscape in "A Vision of April" evades the merely natural order and tantalizes with its suggestive features. The little "grey-sedgèd" brook is yet another version of the stream of life that so often appears in Lampman's work; significantly, the emphasis here is on smallness, dullness, and mortality. The cloud reflected in the water is a more enigmatic image. While it occurs in only one other piece by Lampman, such reflecting images are common in English Romantic poetry. Generally they connote illusion, enchantment, or the danger of solipsism; frequently they are associated with the erotic imagination, which risks the fate of Narcissus. This last meaning proves relevant here.

The speaker discovers a presence in the landscape, a virginal figure surrounded by caroling birds. Only one circumstance is disquieting: she appears amid a "net of tangled boughs," a detail that echoes the entrapment image in the opening stanza. She is sketched in a few lines, yet her implications relative to Lampman's work as a whole can hardly be compassed. Her grey eyes and soft brown hair are further evidence that in some sense she represents Katherine.[21] Her virginal aura implies both the speaker's reverence and his mistrust of sex—an ambivalence that Lampman also expressed through a parallel figure, Artemis, who is explicitly invoked in a later poem about Katherine.[22] As an incarnation of April, this apparition recalls the motifs of maidenhood and Eros conjoined in a number of Lampman's spring and summer poems. In this vision he stresses her ambiguous aspect:

> Like an angel slipped from heaven
>   Or a dryad from the tree,
> Something wide as life was given
>   To her fixèd reverie,
> Something noble, something bright,
> Leagues of summer, leagues of light.
>   (*ALS*, 9)

Lampman invokes both Christian and pagan myths in an effort to fathom the power of love. What eventually becomes clear is that the grey-eyed lady is endowed with light by the poet himself, who projects upon her his own fixed reverie. She is the Lady of his heart's desire, created by imagination; at the same time, she is nature humanized in the landscape of imagination.

Until the eighth stanza the speaker is tentative; then, overwhelmed with passion, he leaps the brook to claim the Lady as his bride. As he tries to seize the vision and affirm its substance, it vanishes. The apocalyptic vision, whether of the marriage of mind with nature, or of perfect lovers, is potent within the boundaries of dreams or art. The attempt to live there is a trespass upon magic ground, and the consequence for the speaker is desolation, chaos come again. Through most of its length the poem is almost purely visual; suddenly the sense of sound explodes into the final stanza:

> For I heard the high roof rocking
>   And the forest clash and roar
> With the wailing wind, that mocking
>   Howled and whistled at my door;
> April was too sweet a boon
> I and autumn came full soon.
>
> (ALS, 10)

April tempts him to embrace a view of nature that is partial and illusory. In the end he is confronted with his own permanently complex, irreducible self, and with the reality of constant change. This vision of April as Lady is also, implicitly, Lampman's most discerning poem on romantic love, a study in disenchantment akin to Blake's "Crystal Cabinet," Shelley's "Triumph of Life," and Keats's "La Belle Dame Sans Merci." It reveals a depth of insight beyond most of Lampman's love poetry. If his Lady turns out to be a phantom, she also represents a guide to his unfathomed self. This was not, however, a direction that Lampman was prepared to follow. In three subsequent lyrics that conjure up the same lovely figure, he reverts to his customary praise and prayer.[23]

If the central crisis in Lampman's relationship with Katherine occurred during the winter of 1895–96, its painful effects lasted for some time. Trying to put the best face on things, he continued to write sonnets extolling their "friendship." This struggle to resolve his frustration gives even the lightest of these lyrics a melancholy undertone, and occasionally—when he waxes glad over some crumb of kindness—an embarrassing pathos. In a letter to Thomson of 30 August 1896, he mentions having endured "a heavy strain of feeling during the last year or two," and as late as 7 October, he refers to "the sore things that keep eating away at my soul" (*CLT*, 176, 179). Of the love poems written in 1896 and 1897, the two most memorable are startling in their dissimilarity. One I take to be a triumph of poetic convention over personal feeling, and the other, a final *cri de coeur*. "A Summer Figure" (c. 1896) resembles "A Vision of April" in relating his Lady's luminous presence to the season and landscape. It differs, however, in a crucially significant way, for the speaker refrains from introspection, holding his attention on his companion with the sole purpose of celebrating her lovely form and spirt:

> Mark ye, how the branches bend
> Round her softly parted hair,
> How the sunshine crowns my friend,
> Tall and slender, straight and fair.
> Hardly shall another be
> Beautiful and bright as she.
>
> (*LK*, 49)

The idealized subject and elegant simplicity are adroitly managed. Lampman's model here is no longer the Petrarchan sonneteers, but a later Renaissance stylist whom he emulates to much better effect. While this grey-eyed lady is the same figure portrayed in "A Portrait in Six Sonnets" and "A Vision of April," she is here given a purely Jonsonian treatment. The erotic impulse is wholly sublimated in a convention, and issues, for once, in a lyric of utter peace and beauty— a poem of summer. "Far Apart" (c. 1897), which Whitridge fittingly placed last in *Lampman's Kate,* is a very different matter:

> Only the dream of you I keep,
> The dream that must be always by,
> The memories that will not sleep,
> The griefs that make me wish to die,
> So far apart, at last, are we!
>
> (*LK*, 52)

No formal convention is invoked to distance emotion when distance is the poet's burden and irreparable isolation his theme. Here the romantic dream is finally acknowledged a curse as the speaker is consigned to darkness, "cast out utterly" by his beloved. If this language reminds us of passages in the Bible and *Paradise Lost*, it can only deepen our sense of Lampman's despair when we recall that it refers not to Adam and Eve in exile, but to Satan damned forever in hell.[24] In these lines Lampman was spiritually at an enormous remove from his glad inversions of Milton's epic in "The Story of an Affinity."

It is notoriously hard to sort out the reactions of life and art in a man's work, but the impact on Lampman's poetry of his relationship with Katherine Waddell can hardly be overestimated. In "The Story of an Affinity" he staked his imaginative integrity on the idea of romantic love, and a romantic debacle in his own life checked—or helped to check—his imaginative development. There is some indication in his last poems that he started to recover, but he had too little time left. If Lampman's personal loss occasioned a loss to us as readers, it is most regrettable. Yet his best love poems, early and late, rival the splendid landscape poems that have largely monopolized the praise of his critics. Lampman's love poetry also presents a fascinating study in complex adjustments between form and content in the late nineteenth-century lyric. It reflects the enduring power of a central Romantic myth. And it does, indeed, constitute "the plot of an intense personal drama" that will still move readers who follow its broken course from illusion, through conflict and recognition, to release.

Chapter Seven
Last Poems

Lampman wrote comparatively little in the final two years of his life. While he continued to prepare the manuscript of his "Alcyone" volume, all but one of the poems that it contains were written before 1896. His letters through that year and into the following January refer to a lack of time and solitude, increased work at his department, and care for his ailing father, who spent his last year with Lampman and died on 11 March 1897. Lampman's own remaining time was to be interrupted by bouts of illness and long periods of incapacitation. In his letter to Thomson of 30 August 1896, he assessed the effect on his poetry of having suffered "such a heavy strain of feeling during the last year or two": "I think all the practical ambition and I am sure all the vanity have been taken out of me. . . . I intend to write such poetry as I naturally can or as I feel impelled to, but I am not going to worry myself about publishing it. I am satisfied if those whose opinion I really value, such as yourself, give me their approval and encouragement" (*CLT,* 176–77). What Lampman did write subsequently is of mixed quality: some fine sonnets and a few good longer poems, but mediocre sonnets and pedestrian verse narratives as well. With his letters, they indicate an interval of spiritual and poetic recuperation. Ironically, his physical health was in decline.

Eventually, the Petrarchan complaints of Lampman's "late love poems" gave way. In the early autumn of 1896 he wrote his sonnet sequence protesting the oppression in Crete, and in late October he completed "The Minstrel," his melancholy vision of a perfect art consigned to oblivion. Between late November and early January, another series of sonnets gave still clearer signs of recovery. "Temagami," "Night in the Wilderness," "On Lake Temiscamingue," and "In the Wilds" had their origin in his camping trip that fall, and they indicate that this journey into the wilderness became an interior journey as well. In this group of poems Lampman acknowledges and honors the unsettling aspects of nature and the answering impulses within himself. The beauty and energy that he finds in the wilderness are all the more vividly realized for his perception of its violence and loneliness. But despite its forbidding features, this landscape is not completely alien: human beings and their arts have a place in it. The dying sunset in "Temagami" and the fire-ranger who makes his visitors at home in "Night in the Wilderness" suggest a poetic as well as a practical relationship with elemental nature. To express his sense of the primeval, the astonishing oldness that he found in northern Canada, Lampman reaches back beyond the pastoral convention to a mythic sense of light and darkness, rock, storm, fire, and water. In an interesting antithesis, Thoreau had once claimed, none too convincingly: "I love the wild not less than the good."[1] In the fourth of his Temiscamingue sonnets, Lampman affirms the goodness "in the wilds" and exults in it as an expression and a proof of vigorous life.

It is revealing, then, that in two other sonnets written at the same time, he returns to his contrary theme. These two pieces became the second and third parts of "The Largest Life," published in the *Atlantic Monthly* a few weeks after his death. The initial sonnet in this sequence had been composed in August 1894. Alternatively titled "The Soul's Solitude," it is one of several poems written immediately after the death of his son, which had sickened him with a vision of the abyss. In "We are alone," an unpublished fragment written at the time, he had disavowed faith in a divine providence; hence, the solitude pondered in "The Largest Life" I may well have a meaning that goes beyond the problem of superficial human relations.[2] That earlier crisis in the summer of 1894 had brought Lampman to confront hard questions, and the crisis through which he passed in 1895–96 brought him back to them. In "The Largest Life" II, dated 29 December 1896, he arrives at this answer:

> Nay, never once to feel we are alone,
> While the great human heart around us lies:
> To make the smile on other lips our own,
> To live upon the light in others' eyes:
> To breathe without a doubt the limpid air
> Of that most perfect love that knows no pain:
> To say—I love you—only, and not care
> Whether the love come back to us again,
> Divinest self-forgetfulness, at first
> A task, and then a tonic, then a need;
> To greet with open hands the best and worst,

And only for another's wound to bleed:
This is to see the beauty that God meant,
Wrapped round with life, ineffably content.
                              (*PAL*, 300–1)

The scriptural allusion (1 John 4: 17–18) and the explicit reference
to God indicate one of those occasional reversions to a traditional
piety that appear here and there throughout Lampman's work. His
language here suggests that his idea of love is very close to the
Christian concept agape. The terms in which he urges his creed
tempt one to read it as a reflection of his relationship with Katherine,
hence as a repudiation of Eros—the same force that pulses through
"In the Wilds," written only six days later, on 4 January 1897.

That other form of love was too powerful to be wished away.
Nevertheless, Lampman wanted to believe that "divinest self-forgetfulness" was not only possible but inevitable. His belief in the
individual's capacity for selflessness was essential to his faith in the
evolution of a "clearer self" for humanity. That theme, developed
in essays and poems since the early eighties, emerges once more in
the final sonnet of "The Largest Life," dated 16 January 1897.

The optimistic view of human destiny that this sonnet affirms
was attractive to many nineteenth-century writers who repudiated
orthodox doctrines. While it derives from Hegel, Lampman was
probably more directly influenced by Tennyson's version of it, and
perhaps (like Bliss Carman), by Josiah Royce. But "The Largest
Life" III is also reminiscent of Wordsworth's sonnet "Afterthought,"
in the River Duddon sequence, and perhaps this last echo is more
significant: of all Lampman's mentors, Wordsworth had struggled
longest with the harshness of time and the knowledge of mortality.
As a sequence, "The Largest Life" moves from a sense of profound
isolation, through a principled view of human relations, to the
consoling thought that one's part in the ascent of humanity endows
life with purpose and meaning. From our vantage point—or our
disadvantaged one—Lampman's evolutionary idealism may appear
noble, but it can hardly seem compelling. In other moments he was
only too conscious of the contradictions within himself and abroad
that would challenge its premises.

Although he lay fallow over the next eight months, Lampman's
letters reflect his gradually reviving spirits. In May 1897 he wrote
a memorable letter expressing dismay at having written nothing

recently and reproving Thomson for overrating his genius: "However it does not much matter in the long run; we shall all get to the same amplefold of oblivion some day, and in the meantime one has a few [h]ours now and then of pleasurable activity—fine sport in fact—and no harm done" (*CLT*, 184). To my mind this approaches an equanimity more genuine than the unpersuasive reasoning of "Happiness" or the strained fatalism of his letters during the turmoil of 1895–96. On 18 August 1897 he noted cheerfully that he had "written nothing since Xmas, and don't expect to write anything more" (*CLT*, 189). In fact, his eighteen remaining months were to be rather more productive.

Although a number of critics have accepted E. K. Brown's view that the title poem of *At the Long Sault* is the outstanding work of Lampman's last years, its merits have been exaggerated to the neglect of certain other pieces.[3] If any late work might be judged a culmination of his talent, it is "The Lake in the Forest," probably written toward the end of 1897, and first published in the memorial edition. The relevance to this poem of the canoe trip made by Lampman and Scott in September 1897 has been noticed by Arthur S. Bourinot.[4] As Lampman described it to Thomson, their route took them up the Gatineau River into "a little, which tho' little is called the Great Achigan.—a brown watered lake—deep, silent, surrounded by unbroken woods, seldom visited by anyone" (*CLT*, 191). "The Lake in the Forest" is a nature poem equal to any in *Among the Millet* and *Lyrics of Earth,* and while it recalls the genius of those early landscapes, it also projects Lampman's powerful sense of the northern wilderness, presaged in the Temiscamingue sonnets of the previous year. The poem takes the form of a sustained invocation to Manitou, the great spirit of the Algonkian tribes. But if we anticipate a dramatic monologue delivered by an Indian, we quickly learn otherwise: it is a remarkably rich amalgam of "native" Canadian elements with the techniques that Lampman inherited from English poetry. Manitou, we discover, is a presence that can appeal to newcomers in the land as well as to the Indians. If the speaker is to be rightly identified, it is as a consciousness that can adapt its Old World language to its experience of the northern regions of the New World—the voice of a genuinely Canadian poet.

There could never be any doubt about the author of "The Lake in the Forest." While it is one of Lampman's more distinctively Canadian studies, at the same time it renews the crucial Romantic pattern of his earlier nature lyrics. The speaker, who represents all men grieved by the world, brings his silence and loneliness to a landscape that yields an answer to his grief. The remote lake secluded in a hollow of the wooded hills is one of those spaces of spiritual discovery—a "dreaming-place"—so familiar in Lampman's work. The speaker finds and greets the "Spirit of the Earth" everywhere in nature's immense variety of forms and creatures (*PAL,* 313). The most obvious analogue in English Romantic poetry is Wordsworth's homage in "Tintern Abbey" to a presence that "rolls through all things," though the sensuous texture of Lampman's poem is (characteristically) more akin to Keats. The unmistakable verbal echoes of the Romantics are precisely those details incongruous with the whole: "demon laughter," the Keatsian "acold," and cave-dwelling fairies who seem like smuggled goods in the Canadian setting. But these are minor lapses; what Lampman achieves is a series of gorgeous word-portraits as penetrating in their way as the epoch-making landscapes of the artists who led the breakthrough in Canadian painting a generation after his death. The animate wilderness of his poem is much closer to the vision of Lawren Harris and Emily Carr than to Wordsworth's "green pastoral landscape." As in Canadian art generally, this wilderness tends to insist on itself, to resist appropriation by an introspective consciousness. The poet's response is personal, but not individuated in Wordsworth's manner; the emphasis remains on "thy," not "I."

It is a sign of Lampman's maturity in this poem that by far the greater number of its echoes direct us to his own earlier work. It is significant that he begins by addressing a "Spirit of the Earth," and that Manitou remains an immanent power, unlike the "Energy" of "The Clearer Self," which seeks to escape "folds of thwarting matter" (*PAL,* 200). The reverberations of image and mood are too many to list; among the most distinct are echoes of "Winter Hues Recalled," "The Frogs," and "The Woodcutter's Hut." The ten-line stanza with its fixed rhyme scheme and regularly varied meter is a modification of the sonnet, much like the form that Keats favored in his great odes. Lampman had used a similar stanza in an inferior poem, "Between the Rapids," and also in a splendid one, "Among the Timothy." It is an ideal choice for "The Lake in the Forest"; each stanza partakes of the self-contained quality of the sonnet without the sense of finality that persists even in the units of such a finely linked sequence as "The Frogs." The metrical variations characteristic of the English ode endow the poem with its tone of high significance; the complex sentences unfold against the measured cadences and eddying lengths of line to convey an expansive reverence that preserves sensation and perception while avoiding the ultimate oblivion of ecstasy. On its larger scale, the poem has ten stanzas rounding out to a total of 100 lines, appropriate to the "fullness" of its meaning.

The design of "The Lake in the Forest" is very rich. The cycles of night and day and of the seasons are only the most obvious motifs. There are also patterns of height and depth, and of the four elements, that give the poem great symbolic resonance as well as formal beauty. Lampman evokes the extreme moods of the northern Canadian woods, including their peculiarly eerie, even eldritch atmosphere—the quality embodied in the Wendigo legend. However, as in most of his work, he perceives natural decay as not merely destructive, but part of a greater, and ultimately good, Creation. The poem completes its spiral pattern in the speaker's morning devotion, with his sense of the interpenetration of all things. While the language of the final stanza harks back to the opening, it also indicates a momentous change in his awareness:

> O Maker of the light and sinewy frame,
>> The hunter's iron hands and tireless feet;
>> O Breath, whose kindling ether, keen and sweet,
> Thickens the thews and fills the blood with flame;
> O Manitou, before the mists are drawn,
>> The dewy webs unspun,
> While yet the smiling pines are soft with dawn,
>> My forehead greets the sun;
> With lifted heart and hands I take my place,
> And feel thy living presence face to face.
>
>   (PAL, 316)

Only in one or two other poems ("The Woodcutter's Hut," "In the Wilds") does Lampman so wonderfully convey this recognition of a glory in carnal existence; an epiphany wherein spirit and flesh are celebrated as ultimately, miraculously one. The first stanza specifies "thy dreaming-place"; in the end the speaker is given an understanding of his own relation to the cosmos, and assumes his place as brother to the sun. The distinctly Canadian setting accommodates a typically Romantic resolution to "The Lake in the Forest": gazing on nature, the poet discovers his own lineaments and the integrity and divinity of his life.

None of Lampman's other late poems is as impressive as "The Lake in the Forest," though the camping trip that probably inspired it issued in a more unusual piece. "An Invitation to the Woods" is a doggerel spoof of his own serious work and his conviction that nature will rejuvenate the beleaguered spirit of the modern city-dweller:

> You shall waken blithe and bold
> As a cork
> From a bed that is not sold
> In New York,
> You shall thrive and grow no thinner,
> On a chunk of bread for dinner,
> With a jack-knife and a cold
> Piece of pork.[5]

It is one of Lampman's few ventures into manifest irony, and he was surprised when it sold for $25.00 to the *Youth's Companion*.[6] Another poem written at about the same time shows that he remained faithful—perhaps this late in his career, too close—to his imaginative roots. "Yarrow," which also appeared in the *Youth's Companion,* is as obviously Wordsworthian as its title might suggest: a moral rumination in ballad stanza, but on the humble wildflower, not Wordsworth's thrice-celebrated river.

The poetry that Lampman wrote in 1898 provides a virtual inventory of his major themes, with the telling exception of romantic love; however, it shows no definite advance toward a stable poetic vision. He mines old veins, reaffirms old faiths and doubts, and continues to let his mood lead his ideas. Predictably, the largest proportion consists of sonnets. Even in this work of his final year, patent imitation—now often of himself—jostles with insight and original power.

The most highly regarded of these poems is "At the Long Sault: May 1660," which deals with an incident in the early history of New France, the massacre by Iroquois of a band of soldiers under Dollard des Ormeaux ("Daulac") on the Ottawa River. It is, however, a poem altogether out of Lampman's main line of development and it represents a peripheral aspect of his talent, not a new direction or culmination in his work. The subject was commonplace in nineteenth-century Canadian literature, as Duncan Campbell Scott had noted in a "Mermaid Inn" column six years earlier.[7] And as Margaret Kennedy has shown, Lampman's treatment of Daulac as the savior of New France is perfectly conventional.[8] The poem's strength is in its vivid phrasing—epitomized in the famous bull moose simile—rather than in any breadth or depth of vision. It is simply a narrative eulogy centered on a time-honored concept of heroism, and if we try to make more of its imagery we will find that its metaphysical connotations evaporate under scrutiny. The contrast between the beauty of springtime and the slaughter in the woods has dramatic, not symbolic value. The image of a circle or clearing in the forest implies only the "ring" of courageous solidarity among Daulac's men, certainly not that magic space in which the poet's consciousness becomes transparent to itself, as in "Among the Timothy" and "In November." Furthermore, the contrast between the perilous wilderness and the peaceful town with its domestic and civic virtues is very much in the established tradition of nineteenth-century Canadian narrative and patriotic verse that celebrates the retreat of "savage" forests before rising villages. Consequently "At the Long Sault" makes a bemusing exception to the usual pattern in which Lampman sets a beneficent nature against urban corruption, and so affords one more instance of his capacity for contradiction and of the "occasional" character of his writing. The occasion in this case may have been a perusal of Francis Parkman's *The Old Regime in Canada* (1874), which Margaret Kennedy has suggested as Lampman's main source for the historical details of the poem. Or it may well have been a deliberate foray into the literary terrain that his close friend Scott was staking out in poetry and prose: the tragic vignette—compact, powerful, often violent, and generally on a Canadian subject. Entertaining this possibility, perhaps we can feel less consternation about the editorial liberties that Scott took in "improving" "At the Long Sault" prior to its publication in the volume titled for it, in 1943.[9]

The early part of 1898 saw Lampman reaffirm his political values in several lyrics, notably in the ringing verses of "Liberty," written on New Year's Day. His prophecy of social revolution in this poem was followed in April by a sonnet, "To the Ottawa River"—whose "dammed and parcelled waters" (*PAL,* 297) symbolize the subjugation of humanity to the industrial order and the prevailing lust for gold. The poet implies that the basic freedom and dignity of the race survive, like the river, the adverse circumstances of particular eras. In "Man's Future," dated 1 May 1898, Lampman returned to his favorite analogy between the growth of a tree and human nature to posit (once again) an evolutionary view of human destiny. While he still had not developed any definite theory of political behavior, his sense of justice and hope for the future remained firm.

The nature poetry of this final year is largely a reworking of familiar elements. Some of Lampman's last poems are quarried out of lyrics written years earlier.[10] Others, having no single distinct source, are replete with the ideas and images of previous work. "The Passing of Spring" might be taken for a paradigm of his nature lyrics in its recapitulation of the seasons myth of *Among the Millet* and *Lyrics of Earth*. Once more, "dream" implies a vital principle in both the landscape and the poet, in whom it is sustained by memory during the "blind" winter. This sonnet again demonstrates Lampman's characteristic adeptness in the form, especially in its memorable finishing stroke: ". . . The maple full of little crimson knots, / And all that delicate blossoming of the elm" (*PAL,* 296). Another sonnet written that spring celebrates "The Robin"; as in so many of Lampman's poems, the songbird cheers the poet's spirit with its message of natural beauty and renewal. "To the Ottawa" (written in August, and not to be confused with "To the Ottawa River") resorts to a symbolic vein that he had mined for a dozen years or more; and the same is true of "The Sunset" and "The Winter Stars."

If there is a common feature to many of these poems (and here perhaps even "At the Long Sault" is obliquely relevant), it is an elegiac quality. They are concerned with "passing" and "loss," with sunset, evening, and rivers-to-the-sea: death, in short, not love, the central theme of the midnineties. While it is tempting to see in this emphasis an anticipation by Lampman of his approaching death, quite as likely it expresses the waning of his most cherished notions about art and about love. In this regard, one of the most interesting poems he ever wrote is "Last Child," composed on 5 December 1898, but unpublished until Whitridge's edition of the *Sonnets* in 1976. It may remind us of Wordsworth's stanza on "the Child . . . / A six years' Darling" in the Immortality Ode, but the problem that confronts Lampman's "dreamy" son is also an issue at the heart of his father's poetry:

I saw my little man child six months old,
The wonder of his dreamy eyes let fall
To watch a sunbeam moving on the wall,
A little shifting sunbeam, burning gold,
Of mystic shadows full as it could hold
The curtains' lace-work, and a curious scrawl
Of swaying twigs outside, and each and all
Were marvellous to him and made him bold
To stretch his hands out so, a moment rude,
And grasp and try to catch it if he could,
And when he could not, like a baffled sage
With patient eyes and head a little bent,
He pondered as we might at ripest age
In grave conjecture silent and intent.

                                        (*LS,* 174)

The child's experience reverses the pattern of Lampman's sonnet
"Ambition" (1896), in which the poet, through renouncing the
turmoil of life for lyrical dreams, grows "as wise as age, as joyous
as a child" (*PAL,* 295). We should appreciate the charm of "Last
Child" as a vivid picture, and note that it refers to an actual child,
Archibald Otto, born to Lampman and his wife in June 1898. Close
attention will discover certain symbolic nuances as well. We may
recall the sun that frequently presides over moments of aesthetic
fulfillment in Lampman's poetry, and interpret this "shifting sunbeam" as a symbol of aesthetic perception. The intricate shadows
that the child sees cast upon the wall provide an emblem of art,
and more specifically of nature poetry. This shadowy design, reflecting both "lace-work, and a curious scrawl / Of swaying twigs
outside," suggests the curious fusion of craftsmanship and material,
inward power and external world, that nature poetry or landscape
painting brings into particular focus. Hence, the child's effort to
seize the sunbeam and shadows resembles the desire to stop the sun
at its zenith in certain nature poems by Lampman—an attempt, in
other words, to merge dream and reality totally and permanently.
His failure, like the warning chill at the end of "Winter Hues
Recalled" and the mocking wind at the end of "A Vision of April,"
signifies a recognition of the enduring boundaries between art and
life.
    While Lampman had always had a reluctant sense of these bound-
aries, they were brought home to him with painful intensity by the

rebuke that experience gave to his vision of romantic love, both in his marriage and later in his relationship with Katherine. Now almost silent on this theme for two years, he touched on it again in a poem written in January 1899. As Margaret Coulby Whitridge points out, "Even Beyond Music" is probably addressed to Lampman's wife, who played the piano.[11] On this particular night the poet asks her to forbear because the music conjures up an ideal world of unalloyed love: "And points us here in a world of pain / To joy and all its cost, / To the beautiful things we sought in vain / And the things we loved and lost" (*ALS*, 27). Lampman may have remembered the last phrase from Tennyson, or perhaps from a poem by Bliss Carman, but the feeling expressed in this lyric seems none the less personal.[12] In any case, I think that we can see part of the "cost" of Lampman's romantic passion as the merely random harvest of his work after 1896.

Still, that harvest had its fruits. While it is vain to speculate on what Lampman might have done had he not died at thirty-seven, his later poems do attest the survival and even the vitality of his talent. It is fitting, then, that one of the finest of all his sonnets is his last poem, "Winter Uplands," written on 29 and 30 January 1899. It is an evening poem, a superb Hesperian lyric, and for Lampman's poetry what "To Autumn" is for Keats's. Yet it is altogether free of the obvious debt to Keats that qualifies our praise of many earlier efforts. The sibilants of its opening lines create a sense of open, windswept space, and the initial, oxymoronic simile renders the bitterness of the place intense. The same sounds and images recur, marvelously altered in their effect, toward the sonnet's end:

> The frost that stings like fire upon my cheek,
> The loneliness of this forsaken ground,
> The long white drift upon whose powdered peak
> I sit in the great silence as one bound;
> The rippled sheet of snow where the wind blew
> Across the open fields for miles ahead;
> The far-off city towered and roofed in blue
> A tender line upon the western red;
> The stars that singly, then in flocks appear,
> Like jets of silver from the violet dome,
> So wonderful, so many and so near,
> And then the golden moon to light me home—

> The crunching snowshoes and the stinging air,
> And silence, frost and beauty everywhere.
>   (*PAL,* 299)

There is a mature spirit in this poem, one that has tempered its faith with knowledge, and surrendered illusions without yielding to despair. It is greatly moving that Lampman returned to partly forsaken ground, the nature lyric, in his favorite form, the sonnet, and with such triumph, a week before his death. If the power of "Winter Uplands" comes partly from our awareness of the circumstances in which it was written, it comes also from its subtlety of tone and vision. In refusing to attribute a divine radiance to the sunset, Lampman finds its natural light sufficient. The transformation in his consciousness of his surroundings is as gentle yet as complete as the coming on of night: a movement from whiteness to a rich coloring, from bondage to action, from loneliness toward home. The poem gathers together many of his favorite images: the wind that breathes life through his verse, and the stars that measure both his smallness and his aspiration. There is the glimpse of a transfigured city, no illusion but the nurturing of an old and distant hope, and there is a sense of spacious freedom reconciled with an admission of mortal limits. Even loneliness and cold have a savor for him, as they merge with the more familiar beauties of the scene in the intensely felt moment of awareness that is the aesthetic cause and effect of the poem. If Lampman finds no redemption in this natural landscape, he nevertheless finds much: respite, beauty, and an interval of happiness in the heart of a Canadian winter.

Chapter Eight

Lampman in the Twentieth Century: Conclusion

It is a commonplace of Canadian literary history that the Confederation group, led by Charles G. D. Roberts and Archibald Lampman, created Canada's earliest substantial body of poetry. Provided that we include Isabella Valancy Crawford, whose first book also appeared in the 1880s, there is good warrant for this view. Lampman, appealing for a first rate Canadian magazine, declared in 1892: "A country only reaches full national consciousness when it has developed a literature. Our literature is yet to make . . ." (*MI*, 84). He went on to qualify this judgment in two ways. First he noted the extraordinary amount of verse, such as it was, already written by Canadians, and then he reflected that although his countrymen had hitherto been occupied in founding the nation, "Yet, I think we are approaching near to the turning point, to a season of awakening creative consciousness in which such an experiment as the establishing of a powerful magazine might perform for us the midwife's task and place us in possession of a new-born literature" (*MI*, 85). In fact. Lampman and his contemporaries were already in the midst of realizing that promise. Before their appearance, only a few Canadian poems written here and there at scattered intervals have enduring literary value. Narrative and dramatic verse accounted for the best work done by their predecessors. Lyric poetry was largely a bog of sentimentality, conventional piety, crude nationalism, misapplications of the English tradition, and stupendous redundancy, even in the foremost of the early lyric writers, Charles Sangster. The work of the Confederation group is by no means free of these faults, but while it bears an unmistakable resemblance to its English and European forebears, and also reflects some of the confusions of infancy, it has a concentrated vitality and distinction almost unprecedented in Canadian poetry.

Lampman has not, however, had an influence on later Canadian writing commensurate with his merit. The manifold reasons for this fact are neatly symbolized by his death in the year 1899; a full explanation would amount to a history of twentieth-century poetry. In the first place, the concentrated energy and enterprise of his contemporaries seemed to dissipate at about the time he died. Roberts turned to fiction, Bliss Carman to an esoteric philosophy, and Wilfred Campbell to Anglophile Imperialism. Only Duncan Campbell Scott continued to mature as a poet, and in a direction away from Lampman's characteristic work. In the second place, the highly crafted, relatively complex poetry written in Canada during the 1880s and 1890s gave way in the first decade of the twentieth century to the popular narrative verse of W. H. Drummond, Robert Service, and Pauline Johnson. Finally, and of much greater consequence, the advent of modernist poetry in Canada during the 1920s and 1930s took the form of a violent attack on Romantic tradition.

From the distance of half a century it appears that this attack was necessary, productive, excessive, and unfair. It revitalized poetry through dismissing aspects of Romantic art that minor talents had reduced to banality, and replaced them with techniques and viewpoints appropriate to the modern age. At the same time, its perpetrators generally misinterpreted nineteenth-century verse, lumping its finest poets with their shoddiest imitators. In Canada, the modernist reaction against a Romantic poet of the second rank was bound to be extreme. Writing in the *Canadian Forum* in 1933, Leo Kennedy accused Lampman of complacency and conservatism, while declaring of the new movement: "We are principally concerned with the poetry of ideas and emotional conflicts. We have detected, as the Lampmans do not appear to have done, that all is decidedly not right with the world; we suspect that God is not in his Heaven. Uncertain of ourselves, distressed by our inability to clarify our relationship to these and comparative issues, we do not feel superior to circumstances at all."[1] In its misapprehension of Lampman, this statement is almost a textbook illustration of literary judgment blinded by generational revolt. Later generations would rediscover Lampman's value, but in the meantime poetry everywhere was transformed in ways that eclipsed his relevance. The potent influences on poetry in Canada came from abroad, not from the past. Indeed, leaders of the new movement advocated a thoroughgoing cosmopolitanism, in contrast to the balanced view of native and foreign elements taken by nineteenth-century Canadian writers such as Lampman.

The revolution wrought by early twentieth-century writers was in the language of poetry, through the cultivation of irony, free verse, and a colloquial idiom. No one who followed them could resort to Lampman's style, but this fact no more invalidates his art than that of Keats, or John Donne, or the anonymous writers of Middle English lyrics. Modernism generated two strong currents in Canadian poetry: a "realistic" movement stressing speech rhythms and spontaneous form, in which Dorothy Livesay is the earliest important voice; and a metaphysical line epitomized by A. J. M. Smith and A. M. Klein. Neither of these new traditions, however, could permanently submerge the established modes of narrative and Romantic lyric poetry, or prevent unforeseen combinations of any or all of these streams.

  With a lengthening perspective, we are apt to see more continuity in Canadian literature than has often been conceded. The tradition that inspired Lampman has also informed the work of many later Canadian writers. If his high Romantic style has become outworn, his central preoccupations persist among an astonishing variety of poets. Nature poetry remains, as always, a major Canadian genre. Many writers since Lampman also have assumed a visionary stance in dealing with social and political themes. And if the idealism of his love poetry has yielded to more explicit, even savage perceptions, still the relation between the sexual and spiritual dimensions of life remains the central issue.

  The two great formal strategies that Lampman inherited from the English Romantics have also been put to use by twentieth-century Canadian poets. The mythmaking tradition of Blake and Shelley has been adapted by writers such as Jay Macpherson and James Reaney, while Wordsworth's more naturalistic, discursive method emerges in the work of Al Purdy and Dennis Lee. There are also poets such as Irving Layton and Leonard Cohen who move between these modes, much as Lampman did. Of course, these writers all display a degree of self-consciousness and irony hardly perceptible in Lampman. But at the same time, certain poets once associated with the reactionary phase of modernism have lately developed rather Romantic features. In a foreword to her *Collected Poems* of almost fifty years, Dorothy Livesay has emphasized the psychic autobiography and personal symbolism that give her work its shape. And P. K. Page, once among the most astringent of formalists, has emerged in her recent poems as a technically diversified celebrant

of life. These two poets have probed the word "dream" more ob-
sessively than any Canadian writer since Lampman.

If, then, Lampman's direct influence has been limited, he is none
the less significant as a founder of one of the main streams in English
Canadian poetry. In his work and that of Crawford and Roberts,
the Romantic tradition became naturalized in Canada. And despite
his diminished reputation through the 1930s and 1940s, Lampman
has never been without appreciation. Indeed, two leading Canadian
poets spoke well of him during that period. In 1943, A. J. M.
Smith praised him as the best of the Confederation group, while
taking the conventional view that "the greatness of Lampman lies
in the purity and sweetness of his response to nature and in his fine
painter's eye for the details of landscape."[2] The following year, in
a review of *At the Long Sault,* Irving Layton judged Lampman "a
poet of national importance"; and the cliché that Lampman is
"merely" a nature poet began to dissolve.[3] While it is unlikely that
Lampman's poetry will become a model for Canadian writers, he
may acquire more influence as a symbolic figure. Already, D. G.
Jones has included a suite of lyrics spoken by Lampman's persona
in an award-winning volume of 1977, thereby doing for Lampman
what Margaret Atwood did for an earlier Canadian writer in *The
Journals of Susanna Moodie.*[4] Like Moodie, Lampman is a worthy and
a necessary ancestor. He was one of the first writers to care deeply
about developing a Canadian literature and to make a major
contribution.

In appraising that contribution, we should do him the justice of
measuring his work in terms of his chosen tradition, and by the
writers he most admired. The outstanding quality in the English
Romantics as a group is the distinctive fusion in their writing of
intellectual penetration and synthetic power. Whether we call this
aspect of their poetry creative imagination, or mythopoeic genius,
or (with Lampman) "largeness of vision," it illuminates Lampman's
own limitations. His eclectic intellectual habits and doubts about
the value of "philosophy" combined with an ambivalent temperament to circumscribe and fragment his vision. Despite poems such
as "Among the Timothy" and "The Story of an Affinity," he never
really succeeded in resolving his contradictions, whether in personal
narrative like Wordsworth, dramatic myth like Blake and Shelley,
a sequence of great lyrics like Keats's odes, or in some commensurate
form. We can see an inchoate myth in the themes and recurring

images of his poetry, many of them part of his Romantic heritage: the Aeolian harp, the seasons, river and journey, stars, wind, and sun, sunset and evening, heat and light, tower and winecup, garden and city, blindness and dream; but here it is significant that the most crucial symbols are always his most equivocal.

Lampman's aptitude for the discrete lyric rather than the comprehensive opus decisively affected the ultimate character of his work. Of the half dozen volumes of poems he published or planned, only *Lyrics of Earth* has a genuine unity of theme and structure. The vision of love that emerged as his imaginative focus in the early nineties was shattered, apparently, by the adverse circumstances of his actual relationships. During the nineties, his Romantic hope for a reconciliation of the alienated self with redemptive forces in nature gave way to more typically Victorian theories about evolution away from a barbaric past and from the physical dimension of human life. On the one hand, he indicts the city as perverting humanity; on the other, he extols "social progress" as taming the brute in us. Without implying final judgments on the Romantics and Victorians, I think we must draw some conclusions about their respective influence on Lampman. On the whole, where his moral vision has emotional urgency, subtlety, and clarity, it is rooted in Romantic literature. Where his verse thickens toward sententiousness or flattens into abstraction and cliché, the influence is likely to be Victorian. There are exceptions—"Storm" is a banal imitation of Shelley, while "An Athenian Reverie" is a fine poem in the vein of Tennyson and Arnold—but, in general, Lampman learned much from the Romantics that he put to good use, and much from the Victorians that he put to bad.

We should ask ourselves, however, how many poets since the English Romantics have achieved a vision of life that is at once complex, compelling, and clearly unified. Among other nineteenth-century Canadians, only Isabella Valancy Crawford excels in this respect, and her *Collected Poems* are by no means free from anomalies. Moreover, we ought to appreciate the justice of Lampman's self-assessment in his letter to Thomson of 12 May 1897:

I don't think you will ever see any thing more of that "great poet" you thought you discovered in me some years ago; but it is part of your own fault. You overrated me. There never was any great poet, but simply a rather superior minor one, who sometimes hits upon a thing which comes uncommonly near to being very excellent. (*CLT*, 183–84)

In responding to Lampman's main point, we may easily overlook the full meaning of what he says. From his critical essays, we know that he did not see greatness in many poets, certainly not in those of his own era, whether in Canada or elsewhere. And if the modesty of his statement is what first strikes us, we should notice the considerable self-respect there too. It is not a negligible thing to be nearly great, nor to come sometimes within a hair's breadth of excellence. Among those poems that vindicate his evaluation, and that are central to an understanding of his work, are "Among the Timothy," "An Athenian Reverie," "The City of the End of Things," "Winter-Store," "The Story of an Affinity," "A Vision of April," "The Lake in the Forest," and perhaps a dozen sonnets including "On the Companionship with Nature," "Sorrow," "In the Wilds," and "Winter Uplands."

Lampman wrote these poems in a place that offered little stimulation or material support, at a time when poetry itself was approaching an epochal upheaval. The Romantic faith in the prophetic significance of poetry was about to disintegrate in a crisis of confidence that has been endemic in twentieth-century art. Lampman anticipates that crisis in his contradictions, his diffidence, and his eclecticism. If his work lacks the organic unity of a great poetic vision, perhaps in that very limitation it speaks to us. In his wishful thinking, capitulations to despair, recovered hopes, and unforeseen moments of piercing insight he continues to reflect our uneasy purchase on a world convulsed by change.

Notes and References

Chapter One

1. Northrop Frye, *The Bush Garden* (Toronto: Anansi, 1971), 14.
2. Bebe Lampman, "Adrift," *Canadian Illustrated News,* 24 March 1883, 187.
3. Carl Y. Connor, *Archibald Lampman, Canadian Poet of Nature* (1929; reprint, Ottawa: Borealis, 1977), 32.
4. Duncan Campbell Scott, "Memoir," in *The Poems of Archibald Lampman* (Toronto: Morang, 1900), xiv–xv.
5. G. B. Sage, "Archibald Lampman as I Knew Him at Trinity University," preface by D. M. R. Bentley, *Canadian Notes and Queries,* no. 18 (December 1976):8.
6. "The Modern School of Poetry in England," in *Archibald Lampman: Selected Prose,* ed. Barrie Davies (Ottawa: Tecumseh, 1975), 100; this volume is hereafter cited in the text as *SP.*
7. Barrie Davies, "Lampman and Religion," *Canadian Literature,* no. 56 (Spring 1973):45.
8. Letter to J. A. Ritchie, 9 September 1882, cited in Connor, *Archibald Lampman,* 60.
9. "Two Canadian Poets: A Lecture by Archibald Lampman," preface by E. K. Brown, *University of Toronto Quarterly* 13 (July 1944):410.
10. Letter to J. A. Ritchie [c. February 1883], cited in Connor, *Archibald Lampman,* 66.
11. Letter to J. A. Ritchie [c. February 1884], cited in Connor, *Archibald Lampman,* 76.
12. Parenthetical dates given for Lampman's poems are the dates of composition, as far as can be determined from manuscripts and other evidence. See L. R. Early, "A Chronology of Lampman's Poems," *Canadian Poetry: Studies, Documents, Reviews,* no. 14 (Spring–Summer 1984):75–87.
13. Letter to May Blackstock McKeggie, 29 January 1885, microfilm copy in Trinity College Archives, Toronto.
14. Annie Lampman, Letter to May Blackstock McKeggie, 30 October 1887, microfilm copy in Trinity College Archives, Toronto.
15. Ernest Voorhis, "The Ancestry of Archibald Lampman, Poet," *Royal Society of Canada Proceedings and Transactions,* 3d ser. 15, sec. 2 (1921):103–21.
16. Scott, "Memoir," xx.
17. E. W. Thomson, "Canada's Tribute to Her Poet," *Boston Evening Transcript,* 14 March 1914; reprinted in Arthur S. Bourinot, ed., *The*

Letters of Edward William Thomson to Archibald Lampman (1891–1897)
(Ottawa: Bourinot, 1957), 45.

18. There has been some confusion about Maud's age, apparently
stemming from the genealogical table giving her birthdate as 1869, in
Voorhis, "The Ancestry of Archibald Lampman, Poet," 119. In fact she
was born 3 January 1867, as a letter by Lampman to her on her twentieth
birthday indicates, and as a birth announcement in the Toronto *Globe*
confirms (Letter to Maud Playter, 3 January 1887, Lampman Collection,
Simon Fraser University Library, Burnaby, B.C.; *Daily Globe* [Toronto],
5 January 1867, p. 3, col. 2).

19. *At the Long Sault and Other New Poems,* ed. Duncan Campbell
Scott and E. K. Brown (1943; reprinted, with separate pagination, in *The
Poems of Archibald Lampman* [1900; reprint, University of Toronto Press,
1974]), 37; hereafter, quotations from this edition are cited in the text
as *ALS* and *PAL.*

20. Letter to Maud Playter, 5 January 1887, Lampman Collection,
Simon Fraser University Library, Burnaby, B.C.

21. Letter to Maud Playter, 11 January 1887, Lampman Collection,
Simon Fraser University Library, Burnaby, B.C.

22. Scott, "Memoir," xxiii.

23. "Fidelis" [Agnes Maule Machar], "Some Recent Canadian Poems,"
Week, 22 March 1889, 251.

24. "Seranus" [S. Frances Riley Harrison], review of *Among the Millet
and Other Poems, Week,* 28 December 1888, 59.

25. "Comment on New Books," *Atlantic Monthly* 78 (September
1896):425–26.

26. E. W. Thomson, Letter to Ethelwyn Wetherald, 25 June 1889,
quoted in Arthur S. Bourinot, *Edward William Thomson (1849–1924): A
Bibliography* (Ottawa: Bourinot, 1955), 22.

27. The Lampman-Thomson letters have been published in *An Annotated Edition of the Correspondence between Archibald Lampman and Edward
William Thomson (1890–1898),* ed. Helen Lynn (Ottawa: Tecumseh, 1980);
this edition, hereafter cited in my text as *CLT,* reprints Thomson's *Globe*
editorial on pp. 214–15.

28. Helen Lynn, introduction to *CLT,* xlvi–liii.

29. Letter to W. D. Lighthall, 20 May 1892, Rare Book Library,
McGill University, Montreal.

30. The phrase occurs in Lampman's column of 7 January 1893, in
"At the Mermaid Inn," in the Toronto *Globe;* all of Lampman's contri-
butions to this weekly column have been reprinted in *At the Mermaid Inn:
Wilfred Campbell, Archibald Lampman, Duncan Campbell Scott in the "Globe"
1892–93,* introduction by Barrie Davies (Toronto: University of Toronto
Press, 1979); hereafter cited in the text as *MI.*

31. See Barrie Davies, introduction to *MI*, vii–viii.

32. Duncan C. Scott, "A Decade of Canadian Poetry," *Canadian Magazine* 17 (June 1901):155.

33. See Bruce Nesbitt, "A Gift of Love: Lampman and Life," *Canadian Literature*, no. 50 (Autumn 1971):35–40, and his "The New Lampman," in *The Lampman Symposium*, ed. Lorraine McMullen (Ottawa: University of Ottawa Press, 1976), 99–110; Margaret Coulby Whitridge, introduction to *Lampman's Kate: Late Love Poems of Archibald Lampman 1887–1897* (Ottawa: Borealis, 1975), 11–23, and her "Love and Hate in Lampman's Poetry," in McMullen, ed., *Lampman Symposium*, 9–17.

34. "I May Not Love You" appears in Whitridge, ed., *Lampman's Kate*, 31; this volume is hereafter cited in the text as *LK.*

35. Whitridge, introduction to *LK*, 22; Bruce Nesbitt, "Lampmania: Alcyone and the Search for Merope," in *Editing Canadian Texts*, ed. Francess G. Halpenny (Toronto: Hakkert, 1975), 44.

36. "Happiness," *Harper's* 93 (July 1896):309–12; reprinted in *SP*, 105–10.

37. "Last Child" appears in *Lampman's Sonnets 1884–1899*, ed. Margaret Coulby Whitridge (Ottawa: Borealis, 1976), 174; this volume is hereafter cited in the text as *LS.*

38. Arthur Stringer, cited in Connor, *Archibald Lampman*, 193; see also Stringer's "Wild Poets I've Known: Archibald Lampman," *Saturday Night*, 24 May 1941, 29.

Chapter Two

1. "Two Canadian Poets," 407.

2. Charles G. D. Roberts, prefatory note to *Selected Poems of Sir Charles G. D. Roberts* (Toronto: Ryerson, 1936), vii.

3. See Lampman's columns of 27 February 1892, 27 August 1892, and 4 March 1893, in *MI*, 24–25, 140, 269–70.

4. See Lampman, *MI*, 18–19, 37–38, 84–85; the phrase is John Sutherland's in "Canadian Comment," *Northern Review* 2, no. 4 (January–February 1949):32.

5. See also Lampman, "At the Mermaid Inn," 27 February 1892, in *MI*, 24–25.

6. Charles G. D. Roberts, Letter to Archibald Lampman, 18 December 1888, Melvin Hammond Papers, Metropolitan Toronto Library.

7. See columns by Scott and Campbell in *MI*, 17, 119–22, 134–35, 149–50, 331–34, 338–39; also Roberts, "Wordsworth's Poetry" (1892), and "Shelley's *Adonais*" (1902), reprinted in *Charles G. D. Roberts, Selected Poetry and Critical Prose*, ed. W. J. Keith (Toronto: University of Toronto Press, 1974), 271–75, 282–95.

8. Charles G. D. Roberts, introduction to *Poems of Wild Life* (1888), and "A Note on Modernism" (1931), reprinted in Keith, ed., *Selected Poetry and Critical Prose*, 269, 299.

9. Scott, "Memoir," xxiv.

10. Lampman expresses high regard for Shelley in his very early essay "The Revolt of Islam," *Rouge et Noir* 1, no. 4 (December 1880):4–6; reprinted in *SP*, 11–16. Similar remarks on Shelley in Lampman's "The Poetry of Byron" indicate that this piece (preface by D. M. R. Bentley, *Queen's Quarterly* 83 [Winter 1976]:623–32) was also composed at a relatively early date. Lampman's altered opinion of Shelley is given in "At the Mermaid Inn," 5 March 1892, in *MI*, 28–29; in his "The Character and Poetry of Keats" [1893], preface by E. K. Brown, *University of Toronto Quarterly* 15 (July 1946):364; and in his "Poetic Interpretation," in *SP*, 91, probably also written in the early 1890s. Ironically, this last essay appears to owe a good deal to Shelley's "Defence of Poetry."

11. "The Character and Poetry of Keats," 363.

12. "The Modern School of Poetry in England," in *SP*, 93–94.

13. "The Poetry of Byron," 628; "At the Mermaid Inn," 6 August 1892, in *MI*, 125.

14. "Poetic Interpretation," in *SP*, 88–90; Lampman refers admiringly to Keats's letters in "The Character and Poetry of Keats," 363.

15. "The Character and Poetry of Keats," 359.

16. "The Modern School of Poetry in England," in *SP*, 94, 103.

17. See especially Lampman's essays "The Poetry of Byron," "The Character and Poetry of Keats," and "Style," *Canadian Poetry: Studies, Documents, Reviews*, no. 7 (Fall–Winter 1980):56–72.

18. "Poetic Interpretation," in *SP*, 87, 90.

19. "Poetic Interpretation," in *SP*, 90.

20. For an excellent discussion of this motif, see Dick Harrison, " 'So Deathly Silent': The Resolution of Pain and Fear in the Poetry of Lampman and D. C. Scott," in McMullen, ed., *Lampman Symposium*, 63–74.

21. "The Poet" appears in 1893–97 MS Book, fols. 36–37, Lampman Collection, Simon Fraser University Library, Burnaby, B.C.

22. John Sutherland, "Edgar Allan Poe In Canada," *Northern Review* 4, no. 3 (February–March 1951):22–37.

23. Lyric 118 of "In Memoriam A. H. H.," in *The Works of Alfred, Lord Tennyson, Poet Laureate* (London: Macmillan, 1885), 281.

24. Harry Levin, *The Myth of the Golden Age in the Renaissance* (New York: Galaxy, 1972), 8.

25. "The Modern School of Poetry in England," in *SP*, 95.

26. Letter to E. W. Thomson, 20 November 1891, in *CLT*, 25. Lampman probably refers to George Henry Lewes's *A Biographical History*

of Philosophy (1845–46), which went through numerous revisions and permutations during the second half of the nineteenth century.

27. Alfred Austin, "The Poetic Interpretation of Nature," *Contemporary Review* 30 (1877):975. In "The Modern School of Poetry in England" (*SP*, 93), Lampman approvingly cites another of Austin's essays, "Old and New Canons of Poetical Criticism," which appeared in two parts in the *Contemporary Review* 40 (1881):884–98 and 41 (1881):124–41.

28. "Happiness," in *SP*, 108.

29. Northrop Frye, *A Study of English Romanticism* (New York: Random House, 1968), 33.

30. Sandra Djwa, "Lampman's Fleeting Vision," *Canadian Literature*, no. 56 (Spring 1973):22–39. See also Norman Guthrie, *The Poetry of Archibald Lampman* (Toronto: Musson, 1927), 14.

31. "Poetic Interpretation," in *SP*, 87–91, "The Poetry of Byron," 625, and "Style," 59.

32. "Style," 67.

Chapter Three

1. John Macoun, Letter to the Ottawa *Journal*, 24 December 1888; cited in *Archibald Lampman's Letters to Edward William Thomson (1890–1898)*, ed. Arthur S. Bourinot (Ottawa: Bourinot, 1956), 70.

2. "Two Canadian Poets," 409.

3. Daniel Wilson, quoted in Carl Berger, *Science, God, and Nature in Victorian Canada* (Toronto: University of Toronto Press, 1983), 68.

4. "The Character and Poetry of Keats," 361.

5. "The Revolt of Islam," in *SP*, 12; and "Poetic Interpretation," in *SP*, 91.

6. Geoffrey H. Hartman, *The Fate of Reading and Other Essays* (Chicago: Phoenix Books, 1975), 142–43.

7. "At the Mermaid Inn," 24 June 1893, in *MI*, 335.

8. "Two Fragments Describing Canoe Trips," in *SP*, 81–86.

9. Samuel Taylor Coleridge, *Coleridge's Writings on Shakespeare*, ed. Terence Hawkes (New York: Capricorn Books, 1959), 58.

10. Hartman, *The Fate of Reading*, 139–40, 143.

11. William Blake, "Annotations to Wordsworth's Poems," in *The Poetry and Prose of William Blake*, ed. David V. Erdman (New York: Doubleday, 1965), 654.

Chapter Four

1. D. M. R. Bentley develops a perceptive discussion of this image in "Watchful Dreams and Sweet Unrest: An Essay on the Vision of Archibald Lampman" [pt. 1], *Studies in Canadian Literature* 6, no. 2 (1981):188–210.

2. Nicholas J. Perella, *Midday in Italian Literature: Variations on an Archetypal Theme* (Princeton, N.J.: Princeton University Press, 1979), 5–6.

3. See Reinhard Kuhn, *The Demon of Noontide: Ennui in Western Literature* (Princeton, N.J.: Princeton University Press, 1976), 39–64.

4. Henry D. Thoreau, *A Week on the Concord and Merrimack Rivers,* ed. Carl F. Hovde et al. (Princeton, N.J.: Princeton University Press, 1980), 125–26, 141.

5. See Harold Bloom, *The Anxiety of Influence: A Theory of Poetry* (New York: Oxford University Press, 1973).

6. "The Character and Poetry of Keats," 371.

7. Richard H. Fogle, "A Note on Keats's 'Ode to a Nightingale,' " *Modern Language Quarterly* 8 (March 1947):82.

8. "At the Mermaid Inn," 2 April 1892, in *MI,* 45.

9. There are detailed analyses by Desmond Pacey, "A Reading of Lampman's 'Heat,' " *Culture* 14 (September 1953):292–97; John Ower, "Portraits of the Landscape as Poet: Canadian Nature as Aesthetic Symbol in Three Confederation Writers," *Journal of Canadian Studies* 6, no. 1 (February 1971):27–32; V. Y. Haines, "Archibald Lampman: This or That?" *Revue de l'Université d'Ottawa* 41 (July–September 1971):455–71; Barrie Davies, "The Forms of Nature: Some of the Philosophical and Aesthetic Bases of Lampman's Nature Poetry," in McMullen, ed., *Lampman Symposium,* 92–96; and D. M. R. Bentley, "Watchful Dreams" [pt. 1], 190–94.

10. The phrase occurs in Lampman's "The Poet's Possession," in *PAL,* 157.

11. M. H. Abrams, *Natural Supernaturalism: Tradition and Revolution in Romantic Literature* (New York: Norton 1971), 447.

12. M. H. Abrams, "The Correspondent Breeze: A Romantic Metaphor," *Kenyon Review* 19 (Winter 1957):116.

13. For an account of the tortuous publication history of *Lyrics of Earth,* see D. M. R. Bentley, introduction to *Lyrics of Earth (1895)* (Ottawa: Tecumseh, 1978), 1–20.

14. "Vision" was published in "At the Mermaid Inn," 19 November 1892, in *MI,* 191–92.

15. D. M. R. Bentley, "The Same Unnamed Delight: Lampman's Essay on Happiness and *Lyrics of Earth,*" *Essays on Canadian Writing,* no. 5 (Fall 1976):32.

16. Harold Bloom, *The Ringers in the Tower: Studies in Romantic Tradition* (Chicago: Phoenix Books, 1971), 231.

Chapter Five

1. There have been few substantial discussions of Lampman's "social" poetry. The best are F. W. Watt, "The Masks of Archibald Lampman,"

University of Toronto Quarterly 27 (January 1958):169–84; and Barrie Davies, "Lampman: Radical Poet of Nature," *English Quarterly* 4 (Spring 1971):33–43.

2. Percy Bysshe Shelley, "A Defence of Poetry," in *Shelley's Poetry and Prose,* ed. Donald H. Reiman and Sharon B. Powers (New York: Norton Critical Editions, 1977), 508.

3. Blake, "Satiric Verses and Epigrams," in Erdman, ed., *Poetry and Prose,* 502.

4. See Reginald Harvey Griffith, "The Progress Pieces of the Eighteenth Century," *Texas Review* 5 (1920):218–33.

5. Abrams, *Natural Supernaturalism,* 334.

6. See Lampman's remarks on Shelley in "The Revolt of Islam," in *SP,* 14, and on Wordsworth and Coleridge in "Untitled Essay on Socialism," in *SP,* 54.

7. "The Character and Poetry of Keats," 359.

8. Letter to E. W. Thomson, 26 October 1894, in *CLT,* 127.

9. Desmond Pacey, "Archibald Lampman," in *Ten Canadian Poets: A Group of Biographical and Critical Essays* (Toronto: Ryerson, 1958), 139.

10. F. W. Watt, "Literature of Protest," in *Literary History of Canada: Canadian Literature in English,* ed. Carl F. Klinck, 2d ed. (Toronto: University of Toronto Press, 1976), 1:478.

11. Scott, "Memoir," xxii; part of the obituary in the *Journal,* 10 February 1899, is reprinted in the Whitridge introduction to *PAL,* xviii–xix.

12. Davies, introduction to *SP,* 1. Davies speculates that Lampman composed this essay between 1885 and 1887; however, the draft in P. A. C. Notebook 15, 2500–13, indicates that it may have been written much later, c. 1895–96 (this and all other notebooks cited are in the Lampman Papers, MG 29 D59, Public Archives of Canada, Ottawa).

13. "Untitled Essay on Socialism," in *SP,* 51.

14. "At the Mermaid Inn," 16 July 1892, in *MI,* 114; see also the columns of 24 September 1892 and 15 April 1893; and "Happiness," in *SP,* 105–10.

15. "At the Mermaid Inn," 24 September 1892, in *MI,* 157.

16. "The Poetry of Byron," 628; and "The Modern School of Poetry in England," in *SP,* 98.

17. "Happiness," in *SP,* 107.

18. W. E. Collin linked "The City of the End of Things" to Thomson's poem in "Archibald Lampman," *University of Toronto Quarterly* 4 (October 1934):114; John Sutherland emphasized its debt to Poe in "Edgar Allan Poe in Canada," 30–31. I have found especially suggestive the comments on Lampman's poem by Northrop Frye, *Bush Garden,* 168; and Eli Mandel, *Another Time* (Erin, Ont.: Press Porcepic, 1977), 117–18.

19. Byron, *Manfred*, III.iii; Shelley, "Prince Athanase," I.26–34, and "Julian and Maddalo," 96–137. Coleridge's memorable line in "To William Wordsworth" has a similar nuance: "the dread watch-tower of man's absolute self."

20. "Emancipation," in "Twenty-Five Fugitive Poems by Archibald Lampman," ed. L. R. Early, *Canadian Poetry: Studies, Documents, Reviews*, no. 12 (Spring–Summer 1983):56.

21. Morris's influence has been noted by E. K. Brown, introduction to *ALS*, xxi, and a number of others. No one has examined at length the close relation between the two works. Lampman evidently changed his opinion of Morris from the thoroughly dim view taken in his early essay, "The Modern School of Poetry in England," in *SP*, 102–3.

22. Collin, "Archibald Lampman," 112; and Munro Beattie, "Archibald Lampman," in *Our Living Tradition*, 1st ser., ed. Claude T. Bissell (Toronto: University of Toronto Press, 1957), 76.

23. The similarity to Samuel Butler's *Erewhon* has been pointed out by Brown, introduction to *ALS*, xxi, and by Djwa, "Lampman's Fleeting Vision," 30. Earlier, Shelley had depicted mouldering thrones and prisons as relics of the wretched ages passed away in the apocalypse of *Prometheus Unbound*, III.iv. 164–89.

24. Blake, *Jerusalem*, plate 97; compare Shelley, *Prometheus Unbound*, III.iii. 34–39.

25. Harrison, " 'So Deathly Silent,' " 72.

Chapter Six

1. E. K. Brown, "Lampman and His Lady, as Told to Me by D. C. Scott," 11 August 1942, E. K. Brown Papers, 2:521, MG 30 D 61, Public Archives of Canada, Ottawa.

2. Duncan Campbell Scott, Letter to E. K. Brown, 28 November 1942, in *Some Letters of Duncan Campbell Scott, Archibald Lampman, and Others*, ed. Arthur S. Bourinot (Ottawa: Bourinot, 1959), 21.

3. Compare Matthew Arnold's "A Dream" (1853).

4. See in particular the two lyrics titled "Sorrow," written in October 1895 (*PAL*, 281), and August 1896 (*PAL*, 309); also "David and Abigail" (*PAL*, 406–7), "The Story of an Affinity" (*PAL*, 461), "Ingvi and Alf" (*PAL*, 355–56), "Magic" (*LK*, 32), and "A Summer Dream" (*LK*, 41).

5. See Lampman's comments on love poems by Rossetti and Swinburne in "The Modern School of Poetry in England," in *SP*, 97, 100; on poems by Charles G. D. Roberts and G. F. Cameron in "Two Canadian Poets," 417–18, 422; and on "La Belle Dame Sans Merci" in "The Character and Poetry of Keats," 371.

6. See Lampman, "At the Mermaid Inn," 9 April 1892 and 27 August 1892, in *MI*, 47–48, 138.

7. Honorable exceptions: Djwa, "Lampman's Fleeting Vision," 30–31; and Davies, "The Forms of Nature," 84–85.

8. The most serious apparent flaw in "The Story of an Affinity," the disproportionate brevity of Part II, is probably due to Scott's editing. The fair copy ms in the Library of Parliament, Ottawa, contains 251 lines omitted from the version published in *PAL*. Part II has suffered the most extensive cuts, 171 lines, or about one quarter of its length in manuscript.

9. The phrase is M. H. Abrams's, in *Natural Supernaturalism*, 141; see also Karl Kroeber, *Romantic Narrative Art* (Madison, Wisc.: University of Wisconsin Press, 1960), 103; and Bloom, *Ringers in the Tower*, 3–35.

10. Poems by Lampman and Crawford, including excerpts from "Malcolm's Katie," were anthologized together as early as 1889, in *Songs of the Great Dominion*, ed. W. D. Lighthall. In 1893 Lampman sent Thomson a copy of *Later Canadian Poems*, ed. J. E. Wetherell, in which some of his own work and a couple of Crawford's lyrics were included; in his letter of thanks, Thomson refers familiarly to Crawford's work and approves "a sort of William Blake feeling in it that is good" (*CLT*, 81–83).

11. Compare Milton, *Paradise Lost*, X. 958–61.

12. Frederick L. Beaty, *Light From Heaven: Love in British Romantic Literature* (DeKalb: Northern Illinois University Press, 1971), xvi–xvii.

13. Djwa, "Lampman's Fleeting Vision," 28; Nesbitt, "Lampmania," 46.

14. See especially Lampman's letters of 30 September 1895, 11 February 1896, 30 August 1896, and 7 October 1896 (*CLT*, 151–52, 163–65, 176–77, 179).

15. Duncan Campbell Scott, Letter to E. K. Brown, 22 August 1944, in *Some Letters*, 40.

16. Duncan Campbell Scott, introduction to *Lyrics of Earth, Sonnets, and Ballads*, by Archibald Lampman (Toronto: Musson, 1925), 38.

17. Duncan Campbell Scott, Letter to E. K. Brown, 18 January 1943, in *Some Letters*, 22.

18. Whitridge, "Love and Hate in Lampman's Poetry," 16.

19. Whitridge, introduction to *LK*, 22.

20. Ms Poems and Notes 1894–99, 1033–35, Lampman Papers, II, P.A.C.

21. These physical features are also mentioned in "Cloud and Sun" (1895), in *ALS*, 25; "A Portrait in Six Sonnets" I, III, IV (1895–99), in *ALS*, 43–44; "Old Indeed are You" (1896?), in *LK*, 47; and "A Summer Figure" (c. 1896), in *LK*, 48. A possible literary model for Lampman's vision appears in Dante, *Purgatorio*, xxviii.

22. "A Summer Figure" (c. 1896), in *LK*, 49.

23. "Spring Promise" (1896), in *LK*, 46; "A Summer Figure" (c. 1896), in *LK*, 48; "A Summer Dream" (c. 1896), in *LK*, 41.

24. Rev. 12: 7–9; *Paradise Lost*, I. 37. Lampman also appears to echo Milton's Satan in another poem of 1897 in which he seeks to come to terms with his separation from his beloved: "All is not hopeless yet, nor lost . . ." ("Gold and Dross," in *LK*, 1. 51); compare *Paradise Lost*, I. 105–6.

Chapter Seven

1. Henry David Thoreau, *Walden and Civil Disobedience*, ed. Owen Thomas (New York: Norton, 1966), 140.

2. "We are alone" appears in P.A.C. Notebook 22, inversed 3297.

3. Brown, introduction to *ALS*, xxii–xxiv; see also Whitridge, introduction to *PAL*, xxvii–xxviii.

4. Bourinot, ed., *Archibald Lampman's Letters to Edward William Thomson*, 40.

5. "Twenty-Five Fugitive Poems," 67.

6. Letter to E. W. Thomson, 2 November 1897, in *CLT*, 195.

7. Scott, "At the Mermaid Inn," 9 April 1892, in *MI*, 48. George Murray's "How Canada Was Saved (May 1660)" had been anthologized with some of Lampman's early lyrics in *Songs of the Great Dominion* (1889), and Lampman perhaps knew Wilfred Campbell's play "Daulac" (see *CLT*, 186–87).

8. Margaret Kennedy, "Lampman and the Canadian Thermopylae: 'At the Long Sault: May, 1660,' " *Canadian Poetry: Studies, Documents, Reviews*, no. 1 (Fall–Winter 1977):54–59.

9. See Scott, Letters to E. K. Brown, [Autumn 1942], 31 October 1942, 13 November 1942, in *Some Letters*, 17–20.

10. Compare "Man's Future" (1898), in *ALS*, 34, with "Man and Nature," stanza 6 (c. 1890), in *ALS*, 13; and "Winter Uplands" (1899), in *PAL*, 299, with "Winter-Solitude" (1893), in *ALS*, 21.

11. Whitridge, introduction to *PAL*, xvi.

12. See Tennyson, "In Memoriam A. H. H.," i, stanza 4 (1850); and Carman, "A Northern Vigil," stanza 11, in *Low Tide on Grand Pré* (1893).

Chapter Eight

1. Leo Kennedy, "Canadian Writers of the Past—V: Archibald Lampman," *Canadian Forum* 13 (May 1933):303.

2. A. J. M. Smith, introduction to *The Book of Canadian Poetry: A Critical and Historical Anthology*, 1st ed. (Toronto: Gage, 1943), 16.

3. I. P. L. [Irving Layton], review of *At the Long Sault,* by Archibald Lampman, *First Statement* 2, no. 5 (March 1944):16.

4. D. G. Jones, "Kate, These Flowers (The Lampman Poems)," in *Under the Thunder the Flowers Light Up the Earth* (Toronto: Coach House, 1977), 74–87; see also Jones's comments on "Lampman's Achievement," in McMullen, ed., *Lampman Symposium,* 115–20.

Selected Bibliography

PRIMARY SOURCES

1. Poetry

Among the Millet, and Other Poems. Ottawa: Durie, 1888.

Lyrics of Earth. Boston: Copeland & Day, 1895. Rev. ed. Edited by D. M. R. Bentley. Ottawa: Tecumseh, 1978.

Alcyone. Ottawa: Ogilvy, 1899.

The Poems of Archibald Lampman. Edited by Duncan Campbell Scott. Memorial Edition. Toronto: Morang, 1900. Reprint. *The Poems of Archibald Lampman.* Introduction by Margaret Coulby Whitridge. Toronto: University of Toronto Press, 1974.

Lyrics of Earth, Sonnets, and Ballads. Edited by Duncan Campbell Scott. Toronto: Musson, 1925.

At the Long Sault and Other New Poems. Foreword by Duncan Campbell Scott. Introduction by E. K. Brown. Toronto: Ryerson, 1943. Reprinted in *The Poems of Archibald Lampman.* Introduction by Margaret Coulby Whitridge. Toronto: University of Toronto Press, 1974.

The City of the End of Things. Edited by Michael Gnarowski. Montreal: Golden Dog, 1972.

Lampman's Kate: Late Love Poems of Archibald Lampman, 1887–1897. Edited by Margaret Coulby Whitridge. Ottawa: Borealis, 1975.

Lampman's Sonnets 1884–1899. Edited by Margaret Coulby Whitridge. Ottawa: Borealis, 1976.

"Twenty-Five Fugitive Poems by Archibald Lampman." Edited by L. R. Early. *Canadian Poetry: Studies, Documents, Reviews,* no. 12 (Spring–Summer 1983):46–70.

2. Prose

"The Revolt of Islam." *Rouge et Noir* 1, no. 4 (December 1880):4–6. Reprinted in *Archibald Lampman: Selected Prose* (1975).

"Friendship." *Rouge et Noir* 2, no. 1 (February 1881):6–7. Reprinted in *Archibald Lampman: Selected Prose* (1975).

"College Days among Ourselves." *Rouge et Noir* 3, no. 1 (February 1882):7–8.

"German Patriotic Poetry." *Rouge et Noir* 3, no. 2 (March 1882):4–6.

"College Days among Ourselves." *Rouge et Noir* 3, no. 2 (March 1882):6–8.

164

"Fishing in Rice Lake." *Forest and Stream,* 10 August 1882, 28–29.

"College Days among Ourselves." *Rouge et Noir* 3, no. 4 (November 1882):4–5.

"College Days among Ourselves." *Rouge et Noir* 4, no. 2 (February 1883):5–6.

"Gambetta." *Rouge et Noir* 4, no. 5 (July 1883):5–10.

"Hans Fingerhut's Frog Lesson." *Man* 1 (November 1885):6–10. Reprinted in *Archibald Lampman: Selected Prose* (1975).

Review of *Lyrical Translations,* by Charles J. Parham. *Week,* 8 December 1887, 22.

Review of *Old Man Savarin and Other Stories,* by Edward William Thomson. *Week,* 9 August 1895, 880–1.

"Happiness." *Harper's* 93 (July 1896):309–12. Reprinted in *Archibald Lampman: Selected Prose* (1975).

"Two Canadian Poets: A Lecture by Archibald Lampman." Preface by E. K. Brown. *University of Toronto Quarterly* 13 (July 1944):406–23.

"The Character and Poetry of Keats." Preface by E. K. Brown. *University of Toronto Quarterly* 15 (June 1946):356–72.

Archibald Lampman's Letters to Edward William Thomson (1890–1898). Edited by Arthur S. Bourinot. Ottawa: Bourinot, 1956.

At the Mermaid Inn, Conducted by A. Lampman, W. W. Campbell, Duncan C. Scott. Edited by Arthur S. Bourinot. Ottawa: Bourinot, 1958.

Archibald Lampman: Selected Prose. Edited by Barrie Davies. Ottawa: Tecumseh, 1975. Includes several hitherto unpublished items: "The Fairy Fountain," "Untitled Essay on Socialism," "Two Fragments Describing Canoe Trips," "Poetic Interpretation," and "The Modern School of Poetry in England."

"The Poetry of Byron." Preface by D. M. R. Bentley. *Queen's Quarterly* 83 (Winter 1976):623–32.

At the Mermaid Inn: Wilfred Campbell, Archibald Lampman, Duncan Campbell Scott in the "Globe" 1892–93. Introduction by Barrie Davies. Toronto: University of Toronto Press, 1979.

An Annotated Edition of the Correspondence between Archibald Lampman and Edward William Thomson (1890–1898). Edited by Helen Lynn. Ottawa: Tecumseh, 1980.

"Style." Edited by Sue Mothersill. *Canadian Poetry: Studies, Documents, Reviews,* no. 7 (Fall–Winter 1980):56–72.

SECONDARY SOURCES

1. Bibliography and Chronology

Early, L. R. "A Chronology of Lampman's Poems." *Canadian Poetry: Studies, Documents, Reviews,* no. 14 (Spring–Summer 1984):75–87.

Greig, Peter. "A Check List of Lampman Manuscript Material in the Douglas Library Archives." *Douglas Library Notes* 15, no. 3 (Winter 1967):8–16, and 16, no. 1 (Autumn 1967):12–27.

Whitridge, Margaret Coulby. "The Lampman Manuscripts: A Brief Guide." In *The Lampman Symposium,* edited by Lorraine McMullen, 131–36. Ottawa: University of Ottawa Press, 1976.

Wicken, George. "Archibald Lampman: An Annotated Bibliography." In *The Annotated Bibliography of Canada's Major Authors,* edited by Robert Lecker and Jack David, 2:97–146. Downsview, Ont.: ECW, 1980.

2. Books and Parts of Books

Addresses Delivered at the Dedication of the Archibald Lampman Memorial Cairn at Morpeth, Ontario. Foreword by W. Sherwood Fox. London, Canada: Canadian Authors' Association, Western Ontario Branch, 1930. Brief tributes by Arthur Stringer, D. C. Scott, and others.

Beattie, Munro. "Archibald Lampman." In *Our Living Tradition,* edited by Claude T. Bissell, 63–88. 1st ser. Toronto: University of Toronto Press, 1957. Biographical interpretation, with a seminal reading of the nature poems as reflecting Lampman's "duality of temperament."

Bourinot, Arthur S., ed. *Edward William Thomson (1849–1924): A Bibliography With Notes and Some Letters.* Ottawa: Bourinot, 1955. Useful information about Lampman's great friend and confidant.

————, ed. *Some Letters of Duncan Campbell Scott, Archibald Lampman, and Others.* Ottawa: Bourinot, 1959. Includes correspondence between Scott and E. K. Brown about their editing of *At the Long Sault.*

Brown, E. K. *On Canadian Poetry.* 2d ed. 1944. Reprint. Ottawa: Tecumseh, 1973, 88–118. Offers an account of Lampman's development, stressing his artistry and his movement toward poems of "human life."

Connor, Carl Y. *Archibald Lampman, Canadian Poet of Nature.* Foreword by Ray Palmer Baker. 1929. Reprint. Ottawa: Borealis, 1977. The pioneering biography; still useful on the life, though insubstantial on the work.

Early, L. R. "Archibald Lampman (1861–1899)." In *Canadian Writers and Their Works,* edited by Robert Lecker, Jack David, Ellen Quigley, 2:135–85. Poetry Series. Downsview, Ont.: ECW, 1983. Includes a discussion of Lampman scholarship and criticism from 1888 to 1980.

Gnarowski, Michael, ed. *Archibald Lampman.* Toronto: Ryerson, 1970. Reprints most of the important reviews and essays from 1881 to 1958, including studies by Leo Kennedy, W. E. Collin, John Sutherland, Louis Dudek, and F. W. Watt.

Guthrie, Norman. *The Poetry of Archibald Lampman.* Toronto: Musson, 1927. A rather slight monograph, with some cogent remarks on Lampman's use of the term "dream."

Jones, D. G. *Butterfly on Rock: A Study of Themes and Images in Canadian Literature.* Toronto: University of Toronto Press, 1970, 96–102. Concise observations on some of the basic ideas and vocabulary in Lampman's poetry.

Keith, W. J. "Archibald Lampman." In *Profiles in Canadian Literature,* edited by Jeffrey M. Heath, 1:17–24. Toronto: Dundurn, 1980. A brief evaluation, with good analyses of "Morning on the Lièvre" and "In November."

McMullen, Lorraine, ed. *The Lampman Symposium.* Ottawa: University of Ottawa Press, 1976. A variety of general and closely focused readings, including studies by Margaret Coulby Whitridge, Dick Harrison, Barrie Davies, and Bruce Nesbitt.

Nesbitt, Bruce. "Lampmania: Alcyone and the Search for Merope." In *Editing Canadian Texts,* edited by Francess G. Halpenny, 33–48. Proceedings of a Conference on Editorial Problems. University of Toronto, November 1972. Toronto: Hakkert, 1975. Reveals the textual corruption in the standard editions of Lampman's poems.

Pacey, Desmond. *Ten Canadian Poets.* Toronto: Ryerson, 1958, 114–40. A fine general essay, relating Lampman's contradictions to his personal circumstances and the temper of his times.

Smith, A. J. M. Introduction to *The Book of Canadian Poetry.* 1st ed. Toronto: Gage, 1943, 15–17. An assessment by one of the leading Canadian modernists, affirming Lampman's achievement as a nature poet.

Woodcock, George, ed. *Colony and Confederation, Early Canadian Poets and Their Background.* Vancouver: University of British Columbia Press, 1974. Reprints valuable studies by Barrie Davies, Sandra Djwa, and Bruce Nesbitt, as well as essays on Lampman's contemporaries Roberts, Carman, and Scott.

3. Articles and Reviews

Arnold, Richard. " 'The Clearer Self': Lampman's Transcendental-Visionary Development." *Canadian Poetry: Studies, Documents, Reviews,* no. 8 (Spring–Summer 1981): 33–55. Interprets Lampman's development as a rejection of Emersonian transcendentalism.

Bentley, D. M. R. "The Same Unnamed Delight: Lampman's Essay on *Happiness* and *Lyrics of Earth.*" *Essays on Canadian Writing,* no. 5 (Fall 1976):25–35. Discovers a number of suggestive parallels between Lampman's essay and his second volume of poems.

———. "Archibald Lampman on Poets and Poetry." *Essays on Canadian Writing,* no. 9 (Winter 1977–78): 12–25. Discusses Lampman's principal critical essays, stressing his ethical perspective.

———. "Watchful Dreams and Sweet Unrest: An Essay on the Vision of Archibald Lampman." *Studies in Canadian Literature* [pt. 1] 6 (1981): 188–210; [pt. 2] 7 (1982): 5–26. Argues that a systematic symbolism informs the poems, and emphasizes the relation between Lampman's nature poetry and his humanitarian commitment.

"Comment on New Books." Review of *Lyrics of Earth. Atlantic Monthly* 78 (September 1896): 425–26. Qualified praise for Lampman's second volume, from an anonymous contemporary reviewer.

Davies, Barrie. "Lampman: Radical Poet of Nature." *English Quarterly* 4 (Spring 1971): 33–43. Stimulating analyses of the political poems.

———. "Answering Harmonies." *Humanities Association Bulletin* 23 (Spring 1972): 57–68. Argues that Lampman's work manifests "the iconography of a remarkably consistent and self-sustaining poetic universe."

———. "Lampman and Religion." *Canadian Literature,* no. 56 (Spring 1973): 40–60. Documents Lampman's dissatisfaction with orthodox Christianity, his affinities with Emerson, and the effects upon the language of his poems.

———. "The Makeshift Truce: Lampman and the Position of the Writer in Nineteenth-century Canada." *Dalhousie Review* 53 (Spring 1973): 121–42. On the motifs of quest and alienation in Lampman's poetry and prose.

Djwa, Sandra. "Lampman's Fleeting Vision." *Canadian Literature,* no. 56 (Spring 1973): 22–39. Perceptive remarks on Lampman's "capacity for dualism" and on the shifting significance of his key word, "dream."

Haines, V. Y. "Archibald Lampman: This or That." *Revue de l'Université d'Ottawa* 41 (July–September 1971): 455–71. An explication of "Heat."

Howells, William D. "Editor's Study." *Harper's* 78 (April 1889): 821–23. High praise for *Among the Millet* from the influential American writer.

Kennedy, Margaret. "Lampman and the Canadian Thermopylae: 'At the Long Sault: May, 1660.'" *Canadian Poetry: Studies, Documents, Reviews,* no. 1 (Fall–Winter 1977): 54–59. Relates Lampman's poem to its probable source in Parkman's *The Old Régime in Canada.*

Layton, Irving. Review of *At the Long Sault and Other New Poems. First Statement* 2, no. 5 (March 1944): 16–17. A positive review by the controversial modern Canadian poet, one year before his own first book was published.

Mezei, Kathy. "Lampman and Nelligan: Dream Landscapes." *Canadian Review of Comparative Literature* 6 (Spring 1979): 151–65. An instructive comparison of Lampman's "dream landscapes" with those of a young Quebec poet of the same period.

―――. "Lampman Among the Timothy." *Canadian Poetry: Studies, Documents, Reviews*, no. 5 (Fall–Winter 1979):57–72. Analyzes a number of Lampman's revisions to show how he achieved a more specific sense of place in his poetry.

Nesbitt, Bruce. "A Gift of Love: Lampman and Life." *Canadian Literature*, no. 50 (Autumn 1971):35–40. A pioneering article on Lampman's relationship with Katherine Waddell.

Ower, John. "Portraits of the Landscape as Poet: Canadian Nature as Aesthetic Symbol in Three Confederation Writers." *Journal of Canadian Studies* 6 (February 1971):27–32. Includes a cogent exposition of "Heat."

Sage, G. B. "Archibald Lampman as I Knew Him at Trinity University." Preface by D. M. R. Bentley. *Canadian Notes and Queries*, no. 18 (December 1976):8. A brief, striking reminiscence by one of Lampman's college classmates.

Scott, Duncan Campbell. "A Decade of Canadian Poetry." *Canadian Magazine* 17 (June 1901):153–58. Contains a concise estimate of Lampman that complements Scott's longer studies in his "Memoir" for *The Poems* (1900) and his introduction to *Lyrics of Earth, Sonnets, and Ballads* (1925).

Seranus [S. Frances Riley Harrison]. Review of *Among the Millet and Other Poems*. *Week*, 28 December 1888, 59. The first substantial review of Lampman's poems.

Steele, Charles R. "The Isolate 'I' (Eye): Lampman's Persona." *Essays on Canadian Writing*, no. 16 (Fall–Winter 1979–80):62–69. Argues that Lampman's use of the first person in his landscape poems implies a persistent estrangement from nature.

Stringer, Arthur. "Wild Poets I've Known: Archibald Lampman." *Saturday Night*, 24 May 1941, 29. A grotesquely mistitled remembrance of Stringer's meeting with Lampman in 1898.

Voorhis, Ernest. "The Ancestry of Archibald Lampman, Poet." *Royal Society of Canada Proceedings and Transactions*, 3d ser. 15, sec. 2 (1921):103–21. Some interesting personal impressions by Lampman's brother-in-law, with detailed histories of the families of both the poet's mother and father.

Waldron, Gordon. "Canadian Poetry: A Criticism." *Canadian Magazine* 8 (December 1896):101–8. An early attack on the Confederation poets as "servile imitators"; Lampman, in particular, is given to "the vicious habit of description."

Wicken, George. "Prelude to Poetry: Lampman and the *Rouge et Noir*." *Canadian Poetry: Studies, Documents, Reviews,* no. 6 (Spring-Summer 1980):50–60. Interprets Lampman's *Rouge et Noir* essays as efforts to define the poet's relation to society.

Index